PRAISE FOR *AWAKEN THE GURU IN YOU*

"*Awaken The Guru In You* offers a revolutionary, liberating process of self-inquiry for "guru avoidant" spiritual seekers wanting to accelerate their path of insight and awakening to the divine truth within themselves."

—Christy Whitman,
New York Times bestselling author of
The Art of Having It All

"Russell Scott has walked a path deep, painful, funny, and above all, fruitful. His awakenings and insights pour forth from these pages. The simple approach of Co-evolution and the dozens of practical exercises in this book will set your inner process on fire, empower you and help you build an amazing life for yourself."

—Lawrence Noyes,
author of *The Enlightenment Intensive: The Power of Dyad Communication for Self-Realization*

"*Awaken The Guru In You* introduces a powerful technique called "The Co-evolution" process. In the 30 years I have known the author, I've witnessed its transformative healing effects in myself and hundreds of people. He shares illuminating insights into the character of many gurus (spiritual teachers). While many have great wisdom, Russell warns us that they are human beings who, all too often, fall victim to their ego and succumb to folly. In this book, Russell guides us in a very illuminating and often humorous and irreverent voice, to get in touch with our own inner Guru. Indeed, that is very wise advice!"

—Terry J. Hodgkinson,
author of *Memoirs of a Wandering Ninja – Walking the Path of Enlightenment*

"*Awaken The Guru In You* is a wonderful guide for people who wish to explore their consciousness. Russell's retreats, his one-on-one sessions, and his book, all serve this purpose admirably. I have benefited greatly for several decades now, from the co-evolution technique described in this book. Rather than present any dogma or belief system, Russell guides people to find answers within themselves. I have found a deeper understanding of myself, and have become much more peaceful, calm, and at ease as a result. I heartily recommend this book to anyone pursuing their evolution."

—David Bryan,
Chopra Center Certified Meditation Instructor,
author, *The 7 Principles of the Affluent Soul*

"*Awaken The Guru In You*" brings an updated and enlightened perspective to a lot of tired old spiritual teachings, revealing vital, practical wisdom for modern people. Russell Scott clearly shows how we can empower ourselves as Masters and become part of the solution to what is vitally needed on our planet now."

—Darren Starwynn, O.M.D.,
author of *Awakening the Avatar Within: A Road-map to Uncover Your Superpowers, Upgrade Your Body and Uplift Humanity*

"If you like your inquiry into both the truth of life and yourself with a good dollop of humour and no "b.s.", then you have struck gold with *Awaken The Guru In You*. In addition to that, Russell is a fantastic storyteller and writer which makes the book a pleasure to read. Thus, this book's distillation of Russell's hard-won wisdom supports the spiritual seeker to end their seeking and start seeing. He holds the hand of your intellect (that is sure it is the alpha-knower) and walks it to meet the place where you can transcend the known and see what is true for yourself. I cannot recommend it highly enough."

—Kathryn Jefferies, Ph.D.,
author of Awake: Education for Enlightenment,
founder, Institute for Well-Being in Education (iWe)

"Russell's playful yet purposeful abilities imbue this book. From the outset, he clarifies that this latest publication was composed for those he calls Independent Seekers – individuals who are yearning for a purposeful path, one that brings a deeper meaning to life. In this spirit, Russell doesn't set himself as a guru who will dole out snappy answers to life's complexities. Instead, this book acts as a guidebook so that readers can proactively connect with their innate truths, genuinely interact with others, and offer unique gifts into the world. This book is well designed for individuals who want to make a difference in the world yet desire to do so in concert with others."

—Gary Diggins,
Music as Medicine therapist and
author of 4 books including *Soundwork as Soulwork: Cultivating Wellbeing through Sonic Rituals*

"If you want to know something, ask an expert." Russell's message is different: if we want to know ourselves, we don't need to ask someone else, we need to ask ourselves. *Awaken The Guru In You* presents a wonderfully simple and profound method of self-inquiry that is unequaled in other spiritual technologies. Apply it and it will revolutionize your life."

—Sandra Fiegehen Ph.D.,
C Psych

"Russell Scott has assembled a genuine methodology of freedom in a voice that is clear, original, and authentic. He has done a great service by making available this wonderful body of understanding and inquiry techniques. It's a little deceptive; what you have in your hand looks like a book, but actually, it is a catalogue of keys. There are freedoms and treasures waiting to be discovered. Use these keys and let the unfolding begin."

—Murray Kennedy,
Enlightenment Intensive Leader

As a therapist and a facilitator of Enlightenment Intensives for ten years now and also an ex guru follower, reading Russell Scott's book, *Awaken The Guru In You,* I became very excited with the clarity with which Russell explained in detail each aspect of truth, a direct experience, a spiritual guide, and so much more. Every chapter is filled with inspiring ways of looking at everything I studied in my training to lead retreats. I frequently use quotes and paragraphs from his book to inspire my participants. I highly recommend reading and using this book!"

—Meranda Squires,
Enlightenment Intensive Leader

"Russell Scott critiques the tendencies people have of attributing wisdom to authority figures other than themselves. He points out that religious leaders and self-proclaimed spiritual leaders often ask us to accept their words of wisdom and guidance without question or criticism. This is often a mistake on our part because no one outside of ourselves can say what is precisely right for us. This book is written "…to release us from the prison of religious indoctrination and to offer a superior alternative to the 'dogma guru,' i.e. the real guru within. This book is heartily recommended for seekers on the path of inner awareness."

—Daniel Benor, MD,
ABIHM, Editor in Chief Emeritus for
The International Journal of Healing and Caring

Awaken the Guru in You

AWAKEN THE GURU IN YOU

The Spiritual Seeker's Guide to Inner Peace, Self-Acceptance and Who You Really Are

RUSSELL ALLEN SCOTT

LUMINATIONS

When we gaze
Into the firmament of the night
There is an effect
That only all stars can relate –
That in shining one to the other
Stars do themselves create
And in all the life that's given
Light is just another form
Of love.

—Russell Scott, 2001

Previously published in 2013 as "Awakening the Guru in You: Enlightenment Through Conscious Communication - The Co-evolution Process"

Editing and Proofreading: Heather Embree-Warren and Lynn Grey
Cover Designer: Pagatana Design Service—pagatana.com
Cover artwork: Lejla Ahmedspahić
Book Interior and E-book Designer: Amit Dey—amitdey2528@gmail.com
Publishing Consultant: Geoff Affleck, AuthorPreneur Publishing Inc.—geoffaffleck.com

ISBN: 978-1-7779469-0-6 (Paperback)
ISBN: 978-1-7779469-1-3 (eBook)

OCC019000 BODY, MIND & SPIRIT / Inspiration & Personal Growth
OCC010000 BODY, MIND & SPIRIT / Mindfulness & Meditation
SEL031000 SELF-HELP / Personal Growth / General

DOWNLOAD YOUR FREE EBOOK

Living From The Inside Out
9 Keys to Awakened Living

Go to awakentheguruinyou.com or scan the QR code below.

IS THIS BOOK FOR ME?

If you've just picked up this book, you're likely wondering, "Is this book for me?" I've been in your shoes, standing inside a bookstore, flipping through dozens of books, and wondering if any of them are for me. So, I'd like to save you some time by letting you know, straight off, who this book is for. Then you can decide if it's a fit.

This book is written for folks I call **"Independent Seekers."**

You're an Independent Seeker if, on the outside, you look like everybody else—you talk, walk, eat, sleep, work, relax, earn money, pay bills, wake, dream—but, on the inside, you feel different.

- You're drawn to explore subjects like spirituality, higher consciousness, awakening, enlightenment, self-realization, truth, etc. You'd rather spend time considering these subjects and arrive at your own conclusions rather than blindly take on the beliefs of a guru or a religion. The thought of dogma gives you a rash.
- You've spent many years alone on a meditative path feeling like you're spinning your chakra wheels and never having the "big bang" awakening experience. You yearn to explore a different approach that involves a deeper connection with others.
- You've been banged up a little or a lot in life and feel you've somehow lost yourself. You look back at your childhood pictures and wonder, "Where did that shining presence go?" The self-help books are piled up beside your bed, and you're feeling

slightly self-helpless. You want to try something that really resolves things for you.

- You followed a spiritual teacher and became disillusioned with his/her behaviour. Their dogma was driving your karma and you ran into a brick wall. You aren't interested in being a follower sitting in the back seat anymore and are now ready to be your own driver. However, you feel you might need some lessons.
- You're in your 40s, 50s, or 60s, have experienced a good amount of success in your life and maybe have a family. You feel trapped in the routines, the responsibilities, and the necessities of life, and are starting to believe material success isn't where it's at anymore. The juice is gone, and the round earth is feeling flat. You're secretly asking, "What's the purpose of life?"
- You're young, maybe in your 20s, and the idea of making a lot of money doesn't attract you. You feel apprehension about participating in the consumer culture. There's no allure there. You might say you're a mystic misfit naturally drawn to explore the deeper realities of life and self in the community of others. You were born that way.

To sum up:

You question, you search, you yearn…for a meaning and a truth deeper than what our culture has offered us. You were taught that everything you need to make yourself happy is available by earning money and buying the right things, but you've been disappointed to find that's not the case. Authenticity attracts you, so you're searching for a way of being and relating that comes from who you really are, i.e., a path that's genuine, real, compassionate, and provides a purpose to your life that gives everything a deeper meaning.

Sometimes, you feel alone on the path because you'd prefer to stare into the unknown forever until the wisdom within shows up rather than sit cross-legged on a cushion and be spoon-fed someone else's fast-food version of reality. This is the price you're willing to pay for wanting to live from the place that intuitively feels is the only place to live—your true self. Truth be told, you also need to connect to others and the world in a way that makes you feel you belong to the mystery that's grander than yourself.

If some of these descriptions fit you, pick up this book and come along with the rest of us Independent Seekers. We're here to discover the truth of ourselves for ourselves, genuinely connect to others, and offer our uniqueness to the world. The good news is that it's not necessary for us to be Lone Rangers. Yes, we have to do it by ourselves, but we don't have to do it alone. There are too many of us now. We can do it alone—together—with this revolutionary method of wisdom and awakening called the Co-evolution Method.

So, come on along. I have lots to share, and we've got an exciting journey ahead, together.

Logic
Occult and Psychic Revelations
Dogma Doo-Doo
The Dangers of Dogma
Fundamentalism and Cults
Dogma-Free Zone
Chapter 6: Personal Reality and Ultimate Truth 49
Insight
Direct Experience
Aspects of Direct Experience
Chapter 7: Enlifenment 63
After Awakening
Presenting the Self
Community
Clearing the Mind and Emotions
Practicing Presence
Physical Health
Chapter 8: To Guru or not to Guru? 73
What's a Guru?
The True Teacher
Qualities of an Authentic Spiritual Guide
Chapter 9: The Conscious Seeker. 91
Lean Toward Responsibility
Lean Toward Being Your Own Guru
Lean Toward Your Dogma Detector
Lean Toward the Unknown

Lean Toward Personal Psychological Work
Is There an Alternative to the Dogma Guru?

Chapter 10: Co-Evolution 111

Alone in the U-n-I-verse
My Personal Awakening to Co-evolution
Awakening within Suffering

Chapter 11: Communication and Co-evolution 123

The Decision to Relate
Contact
Speaking
The Communication Cycle

Chapter 12: Co-evolution and the Dyad Technique 131

The Quantity and Quality of Relating
The Dyad Structure
Preparation Before the Dyad Begins
The Co-evolution Process with Dyads

Chapter 13: The Enlightenment Intensive (aka the Coming Home Retreat). 149

What Is an Enlightenment Intensive?
What Is Enlightenment?
The Co-evolution Process in the Enlightenment Intensive
The Steps Leading to Enlightenment
The Value of Enlightenment in Life
A List of Benefits
Testimonials
Our Journey So Far
Mission Possible

Chapter 14: Organizing a Co-Evolution group 173

Procedure

Guidelines for the Co-evolution Group

Co-evolution with the Dyad Technique

Chapter 15: Co-evolution Groups 179

Resonance

The Co-evolution Insight Group

The Co-evolution Truth Group

Common Initial Concerns

Conclusion

Chapter 16: Suggested Co-evolution Dyads. 191

Self-acknowledgement and Self-image

Problems

Acceptance

Innocence

Thought Clarification

Belief Clarification

Guilt and Shame

Criticalness

Love

Enlightenment

Enlifenment

Creating Your Own Instruction

Additional Co-evolution Dyads

Resources 237

Gratitude List 239

Who is Russell Allen Scott? 241

INTRODUCTION

THE FALLEN HIERARCHY

For over 35 years, I've been working with individuals to help them discover their real purpose in life, to awaken to the magnificence of their true nature, and to assist them in dissolving the reactive mind. This allowed them to begin creating their lives from the truth of themselves instead of re-manifesting the same old suffering.

In 2009, I burnt out. I reached a point where I'd been pushing the river too much, so to speak, by engaging in too many one-on-one sessions and workshops. Although I hadn't recognized the degree of my burnout, a good friend of mine did, and she invited me to her villa in Belize to stay with her and her husband for a week to recuperate. I'd been feeling a growing sense of discouragement about how the world seemed to counteract genuine spiritual development and how, in many ways, it labeled spiritual seekers as heady, impractical weirdos with nothing of substance to contribute to the ambient consumer culture.

I was seriously thinking of giving up the task of helping others awaken. I was feeling like I'd put in my time as a personal transformation facilitator, and was I planning on going out and getting a "regular Joe" job where I could experience the no-thinking mental state of working in a multi-national chain store, taking merchandise out of boxes, and putting it on shelves. Perhaps I'd missed the point of life, and re-stocking store shelves was really nirvana. Or maybe what I was really looking for was something to re-inspire me.

So, I went to Belize. I spent a lot of time sleeping and enjoying the sun and heat—a welcome respite from the Canadian winter. I thought my trip was really all about resting, but, on my fourth day there, as I was thinking about going back home and wondering what I'd say to people about what I did while I was in Belize, I decided to do something touristy. At least I could say I did something other than sleep in the hot sun. I decided to visit the site of an ancient pyramid, thinking that the visit would fit into the category of the mystical and satisfy some of my spiritual friends.

I booked a trip to Lamanai, Belize, one of the oldest pyramid sites in Central America. It took us about an hour to boat up the river, as it was in a secluded part of the country in an unpopulated area off the eastern coast of the country.

We toured a number of the smaller pyramids on the site. When I got to the largest pyramid, I was inspired to climb to the top to do a brief meditation. Several other tourists had also made the climb to the top and, for a while, there was a crowd of people looking around, gabbing, and enjoying the view. I thought there was no way I'd get time to myself, but then everyone left, and I was alone at the top. I managed to stand there with my eyes closed, in silence, for about five minutes before the tour guide yelled from the bottom for me to come down.

But that was enough. I felt a vague sense of something shift in me, but I didn't know what it was at the time. When I came down from the pyramid, I found myself walking beside the tour guide and decided to take advantage of the coincidence by asking him about his personal interest in the Mayans. It turned out he had a degree in archaeology and was an expert on Mayan culture.

I asked him about his theory on why the Mayan civilization disappeared (having read different explanations in a number of publications over the previous year, including the popular New-Age explanation that the culture had "ascended").

The guide immediately responded that he believed the decline of the culture was the result of two things: the ego aggrandizement of the emperors and the hierarchical system of religion and governance. He explained that the pyramids were built as monuments to each emperor. As each new emperor installed himself, he had to build over the face and top of each pyramid constructed by his predecessor to emphasize his prominence. To do this, the Mayans needed lime to cement the stones in place. To create the lime cement, they had to burn the limestone in the area with wood from the trees that were growing in the vicinity. As more and more trees were cut and burned and the landscape became denuded, the climate became drier and hotter. Without the moderating effect of the trees on the wind and temperature, the crops failed.

He further related that Mayan culture was based on a multi-god religion, and power was vested exclusively in the priests and kings. The rulers became more and more removed from their underlings and gradually lost touch with the actual conditions of daily life as experienced by the people. Instead of realizing the consequences of their egotistical actions on the environment, they thought the solution was to appease the gods with human sacrifices. The high priests instilled fear in the minds of the people with threats that if the gods weren't pleased, there would be disaster.

For many years, the populace accepted this practice. It was part of their religion. It was part of their culture. They lived from birth to death under the doctrine that had been passed down from the emperor to the high priest to the initiates and to them. They were indoctrinated. What else could they do but believe in the divine decree of the emperor? But, of course, the sacrifices didn't work. There were more and more crop failures, and people were starving.

As food resources dwindled, city-states that had once thrived in peaceful co-existence began to invade one another. Each city-state convinced its citizens that the other city-states were enemies. The conquerors robbed the conquered of food and riches and subjected those they vanquished to slavery. After decades of environmental devastation, food shortages, sacrifices, and war, many of the populace got fed up with the sacrificing of their husbands, wives, and children, and those who didn't starve eventually walked into the jungle. As a result, one might say that the emperors then "ass-ended."

After the guide finished his summary, he looked at me and continued walking. His silence spoke volumes: "Same old history, brand new news."

I was shocked to realize how history was, in that moment, repeating itself. Although I wasn't sure of the veracity of the tour guide's historical summary, I saw the connection. We have environmental degradation caused by over-consumption of resources, deforestation, and the political elite that dictates to the masses and manipulates them to fear their neighbors. We've sacrificed our children to the gods of war in the name of creating peace. We've invaded other countries to secure their resources. We have various religious authorities that have programmed their followers to believe that the only way to heaven is to adhere to their prescribed path.

Although I was aware of this before, it became even clearer to me how easily the political and religious elite can manipulate a population to believe whatever they want them to believe. There are many examples in our own time of how a mass culture can become a mass cult, galvanized around a few charismatic leaders whose oratorical and personal powers are sufficiently advanced to alter people's perceptions of reality—to the point where people will put their own lives in jeopardy to support a lie. How did we come to believe that there were weapons of mass destruction in Iraq? Did we really believe that Jews are an inferior race and must be eliminated?

In the religious sphere, history is replete with examples of self-appointed spiritual leaders promising nirvana and a blissful afterlife, only to lead devotees down a path of mind control, financial poverty, physical abuse, sexual predation, and even suicide. One need not search far to find examples: the death cult of Reverend Jim Jones, the sexual and child-abuse inherent in the polygamous offshoots of the Mormon Church, the multi-million-dollar lawsuits being faced by the Catholic Church related to sexual abuse.

I've always known that behind the pain and suffering of followers seduced by charismatic leaders and teachers, the real sacrificial victim of political and religious dogma is truth. When the tour guide looked at me after relaying his story, it was as if I suddenly realized the extent to which this pattern reaches far back into our human history and still resides in our consciousness.

Why?

The question stopped me in my tracks.

I thought about the years and years I'd spent searching for the truth and employing various techniques to help people reach spiritual realization for themselves. I thought about the 11 years I'd spent running a retreat center, witnessing and participating in events that helped people come to inner peace and connect to their true selves. I thought about how I, too, had been seduced into a cult many years previous and experienced damage to others and myself. I mentally sorted through my file box full of memories searching for the answer.

Then, for some reason, I turned and looked back at that huge Mayan pyramid. When I took in its imposing presence on the landscape and its enormity, the reason for my lack of finding the answers suddenly became clear. It had to do with the way in which the deception is delivered. The problem is the pyramidal structure, the hierarchy: Emperor to priest to initiate to populace; pope to bishop to priest to congregation; guru to chela; teacher to student; author to reader. The idea that one's personal evolution is totally dependent on receiving the truth from another—who's supposedly more enlightened, more advanced, more exalted, and more knowledgeable—is the real problem. Yes, there are other factors involved, but the fundamental problem is the structure—the hierarchical structure.

When there's a socialized perception that those higher up the political and religious ladder are more spiritually evolved, automatically we tend to believe that truth and knowledge are more accessible to those higher up than ourselves. We believe truth is acquired from without rather than inspired from within, and that it's dependent on a teacher's exposition rather than our own exploration. Within the hierarchical structure, people are likely to accept dogma as truth rather than depending on their own discrimination.

At this point, with this new insight in mind, I rejoined the group of tourists and the realization retreated into the back of my mind. I completed the tour of Lamanai and returned to my hotel room for the evening. As I drifted off to sleep, I re-lived the whole scene and began to ponder the question, "If the hierarchical approach is problematic for spiritual growth, what's the better way?"

The next morning, I awoke with the mental image of that huge pyramid rising out of the jungle. The question persisted: "How does consciousness evolve in the most optimal way?" As I sat with the question, my mind was drawn to a vision of the jungle itself, the environment out of which the pyramid had arisen, and the penny dropped. It was simple. I saw it in the nature of the forest itself. I saw each element in the forest: the trees, the insects, the animals, the plants in the understory, and the soil organisms, all evolving together. "Life evolves in relationship."

It was clear that consciousness didn't evolve as the result of one person delivering his idea of truth down the line so that those below accepted it as a second-hand belief. It evolved in a more democratic process of equals relating to one another, and this was far more effective. Just as many organisms in the forest adapted and evolved symbiotically to reach their present state, we, too, evolve through our interactions and relating to one another. We evolve together in an organic, democratic process. The name for this came to me: "Co-evolution."

As I sat with this new piece of the puzzle, a final piece clicked into place: "Russell, you're already leading people through this process."

For the previous 35 years, I'd been leading people through many seminars and retreats using a process where people sat in dyads (two people) or small groups, inquired into personal and ultimate questions of life, and shared their thoughts and experiences. As people related with each other in this way, they arrived at deep personal insights, let go of internal blocks, and awakened to the divine nature of their existence. I didn't teach any dogma or philosophy. I only taught a contemplation and communication technique, and people naturally evolved as the result of practicing it. I'd never had a label or fitting term to explain what it was that I did. But this new term, "Co-evolution," wrapped up what I was doing into a neat little bundle. I found that this new label carried a lot of power—it could easily be understood, and it communicated the immense benefits people were receiving from the method. With this came the inspiration to share this concept with a wider audience. And, I'm excited to say, that's what I'm doing now with this book.

My secret hope is that what's presented in this book will release you, as a spiritual seeker, from the prison of religious indoctrination and offer a superior alternative to the "dogma guru," i.e., the guru within you.

So, just like a young mother, I've struggled through all the challenges and joys of pregnancy and finally given birth. I now recognize the beauty and blessing of what has arrived—a radical new method of opening up to the mystery of self and seeing into the nature of existence.

There's one proviso in all this that needs to be made clear: I'm aware that I'm walking the thin line of paradox. In offering up my wisdom to you about truth, the spiritual path to awakening, and the danger of dogma gurus, I could very well be creating in you another set of beliefs that can imprison you. To prevent this, I ask you to not believe anything I present to you but, on the other hand, not to disbelieve what I write. I ask you to consider this discourse and dwell somewhere in the zone between openness and skepticism, the unknown and the certain, and to treat my ideas as hypotheses until you, yourself, in your own experience, discover them to be true or not. Please try out the co-evolution exercises at the back of the book with fellow spiritual cohorts and base your evaluation on that experience.

My greatest wish is that you become inspired like me and thousands of others by the liberating power of the co-evolution process and that you revel in its naturalness and beauty. I hope you, too, can use it to transform your life and get turned on to the exciting journey of finding wisdom and joy in the most obvious and yet unexpected place—yourself. Maybe along the way, you and others will discover something else vitally important—that co-evolution is going on all around us—inherently in the nature of life itself—and **that the saviour we've been waiting for…is us!**

Chapter 1

HOLY COW HAMBURGER

The guru tradition has been an ancient tradition in the East for centuries. Spiritual teachers have been a respected part of spiritual practice, and their wisdom and guidance have been honoured as an essential aspect of everyday life. Within the Eastern religions, there are elaborate codes of conduct that both preserve the stability of life within the religious order and set it apart from the popular culture. These traditions emphasize the sublimation of personal will and ego identification in favour of worship, service, and conformity to spiritual authority.

But, as these spiritual teachers have migrated to the West—which emphasizes individuality, laissez-fare morality, and capitalism—their messages have been confusing and sometimes painful. Our culture has processed these Eastern holy cows into hamburgers.

The West has also produced its own, home-grown, self-appointed teachers, who are anointed by their own professed divine revelations. They've seduced many of their followers with their charisma and personal power. They've told us their version of reality is the one to believe. Many followers have been seriously misled by abuses of sex, money, and power, and have even been encouraged to commit serious crimes or suicide on behalf of these self-anointed gurus. The practices, beliefs, and rituals of these men and women have, quite rightly, been met with derision, leaving many serious spiritual seekers harmed, wary, and angry at the whole scene.

In addition, we've seen a merging and blending of many traditions into new, creative iterations of practices and beliefs: yoga and aerobics, shamanism and energy therapy, Buddhism and psychotherapy. I've even come across a practice that combined Native American spirituality, kabbalah study, and rebounding called, "Yahoo-ism." The variety of these combinations and the hype around their effectiveness is dizzying. When established traditions are combined with new, untested practices and then re branded with creative marketing, the spiritual consumer has a hard time determining the efficacy and authenticity of these teachers, their beliefs, and practices. Some of these new combinations are untested and dangerous, while others have produced some remarkable improvements over age-old traditions.

We're also experiencing a blending of spirituality and capitalism delivered in over-priced, under-delivered seminars that somehow equate financial abundance with higher consciousness and self-worth with net worth. These movements prey on people's fears and dreams of easy riches, promoting greed while sinking their students deeper into a you-can-have-it-all materialism—and, all too often, debt. Self-help books offer a prepackaged set of beliefs and quick fixes that leave people feeling a sense of self-helplessness, failure, and cynicism rather than deep transformation.

I've personally had both positive and negative experiences with teachers over the years. I've experienced the emotional pain of being part of a dogmatic spiritual cult, and a psycho-therapeutic cult that left me with my marriage damaged and good friends estranged. I've witnessed the harm that results when sociopathic gurus are caught with their pants down, their hands in the till, or their golden shoes fastened to the pedestal. Many gurus have used brilliant transformation methods to scam others for their own selfish purposes. They've led people to discredit genuine advanced spiritual practices and throw the baby out with the bathwater. I've also counseled seekers who've been mentally and psychologically injured because they blindly placed their trust in the dogma and unhealthy practices of their mentors.

Yet, on the other hand, I've experienced immense benefits—including powerful divine awakening experiences—gained under the mentorship of several spiritual guides. These people have supported me with love and firmness. They helped me through barriers on the path that I couldn't have overcome on my own. As well, in my 11-year tenure as the owner of the Ecology Retreat Centre in Ontario, Canada, I've had the pleasure—and sometimes disappointment—of interacting with many spiritual teachers, gurus, seminar leaders, and personal-growth facilitators. As a result, I've been exposed to a wide spectrum of wisdom teachers and spiritual paths, some of whom are genuine and life-affirming, and some of whom are harmful, misguided, and downright weird.

It's no wonder that the whole spiritual scene has come under scrutiny. People are wondering if there's any value in having a guru and following any form of tradition.

Yes, the West has made hamburger out of the holy cows in the guru tradition, and, although it's been disheartening for some, others—like me—have seen the blessing behind the curse. For too long, we've looked on dogma as the necessary evil that accompanies the guru so that we may advance on the spiritual path. *Now we're seeing clearly that dogma is the* unnecessary veil *between the divine and ourselves,* and we no longer want it. Let it be understood that I'm not advising anyone not to follow a guru or to just follow your own intuition blindly without external guidance. These choices must be personal options, but we mustn't make them blindly. There's much to consider even before we make these decisions. I'd suggest that the first considerations are some basic questions, which we'll address in the next chapter.

Chapter 2

THE FIRST QUESTIONS

"For everyone there is a guru. I admit a guru for myself, too. Who is my guru? ...The guru is the Self."

—Ramana Maharshi

DO I NEED A GURU?

"Do I need a guru?

"What do I gain from having one?"
"Can I get enlightened without one?"
"If I do require one, what kind of guru do I need?"
"How can I avoid dogma?"
"How can I recognise a true teacher?"
"What are the conditions for me to become my own guru?"

These are all crucial considerations for anyone on a spiritual path. To guru or not to guru…that is the question.

Before attempting to answer these queries, I propose that there are other questions we need to answer first. These will form a basic understanding from which answers to the above questions can be developed. These are the foundational questions I suggest we consider:

"What's the purpose of a spiritual path?" *and*

"What is a spiritual path?"

It stands to reason that if we know the purpose of the spiritual path, we'll be able to determine what kind of teacher we need to accomplish that goal. We'll be clearer about the path to follow to find the guru inside ourselves. If the aim is to be happy, maybe we just need a person to tell us jokes all the time. If the aim is to be financially stable, maybe we need a business coach. If the aim is to have more knowledge, maybe we require someone to stand at the front of the room and give us lectures. Let's begin our investigation.

WHAT'S THE PURPOSE OF A SPIRITUAL PATH?

Is the purpose of a spiritual path to find greater wisdom, make more money, become more successful and accomplished, become calmer or more energetic, feel more fulfilled in life, gain personal mastery, or something else? Ask anyone who has a spiritual bent, and you'll get hundreds of different answers. And, believe me, I've asked a lot of people. When I ran the Ecology Retreat Centre in Orangeville, Ontario, I asked this question to many people who came there for personal development, and I got a wide variety of answers. I also did my own research—in the course of delivering my own seminars—by asking people, "What's your highest goal in life?" For both of these questions—"What's the purpose of the spiritual path?" and "What's your highest goal in life?"—the answers seem to boil down to the similar things. People state they want to "be all I can be," "live from the depth of my soul," and "live a life that fully expresses myself." They want to be themselves, fully.

So, it seems people feel that the purpose of a spiritual path is to discover the truth of life, the self, the self in relationship to others, and to fully manifest that truth. To distill this even further, it's simply that people want to "be themselves to fullness" or live a "be-you-to-fullness" life. We could also call this true-self-actualization—the complete presentation of our true self in life. It appears that this full engagement of ourselves in any activity of life is what brings fulfillment. When we're fully participating in our work—not from our personality but from who we really are—the potential for success is much greater. When we're fully present in our real self in our intimate relationships, there's a deeper connection with our partners and more love exchanged. When we're fully and authentically present in our recreational activities, we're happier.

You might want to verify this for yourself right now. Go ahead, stop reading for a few moments, and feel the rightness or wrongness of these ideas for yourself. Do these statements resonate with you? How do they make you feel?

Don't read on just yet. Take a minute and think about these questions.

Now that you've considered, think of this: What is it that you're trying to do in leading a spiritual life? Certainly, it has something to do with living, right? It's certainly not about dying. It has something to do with being alive. If that's the case, maybe it's about living a better and happier life than the one you have—to live in such a way that life is more satisfying and inspiring. Maybe it's about discovering something deeper about life that can do this for you. Perhaps there's a non-physical realm that can uplift and inform you. Or maybe the material realm is all there is.

How are we to know what's what?

Well, it seems obvious that if we're to find the answers, we must search for them. We must seek to discover. If this is so, what are we to discover? I suggest to you that we must discover the truth, because if we discover something false and try to live from that, we're going to be in trouble. If we believe there's no food in the house—and the truth is that there's a feast in the next room—we're in danger of starving. If men and women believe that the opposite sex is the enemy, we'll never reproduce, and the human race is doomed. So, we can't live from falsehood. It doesn't produce a better life.

We need to live from truth.

If being uplifted is something we want, we need to understand what life, others, and the self actually are, so we can at least live in harmony with that reality. If fulfillment in life comes from our engagement in it, we need to know what we're engaging in. If we erroneously believe that a river flows upstream, launch our boat downstream from our destination, and hope to get there easily, we've going to have a big problem. If we want to be more fulfilled as a person, it makes sense to know the truth of who we really are and be that. If we believe we're a dog and that some other people are cats, and we start acting like a dog around others who think they're cats, we're also in big trouble. So, we need to live in alignment with who we really are, what others are, and what life is.

Therefore, **the first step on the spiritual path is to know the truth.** Once we know who we really are, what others are, and what life is, there's a great possibility that, on a basic level, we can live in harmony with these actualities.

So, this prompts two questions:

1. What is truth?
2. How do we find the truth?

Chapter 3

WHAT IS TRUTH?

As we begin to investigate this question, all kinds of barriers arise that can get in the way. We can feel an aversion to the truth. We can look at the term as one of those profane "four-letter" words, even though it has five letters. The word itself can become associated in our minds with all the so-called truth purveyors who've deceived people with a version of reality that was, in the end, a pack of lies. Millions of people have been killed and hurt in the name of truth. We can get cynical and suspicious of this investigation. We can get entangled and lost in a maze of philosophical investigations about the nature of truth and not find our way out for years. We could decide that truth just can't be known and give up.

It isn't necessary to engage in any of this. Really. There's a simple definition. Over the years and years of being a fanatic at truth-seeking, to my embarrassment, I missed the obviousness of its definition.

Are you ready for the shock of its utter simplicity? Are you ready to smack your head and say, "Duh!"

The truth is the way reality actually is.

Yes, it's that simple.

Let's explore this more deeply.

THE WAY IT ACTUALLY IS

The truth isn't the way we want things to be, the way others view life, the way we feel about something subjectively, the way we define things through our concepts or beliefs, or the way we want, affirm, or imagine things to be. It's none of these things. The truth is the actuality of life, self, and others. It's the fact of something, its essence.

There's the way we think, believe, feel, affirm, perceive, or hope things are, and then there's the way things—meaning the realities of self, life, and others–actually are. Ultimately, any thoughts we come up with about these realities of self, life, or others are just that—ideas. Ideas are conceptualizations and, as such, are just pictures in the mind; they aren't the real things. When we think of the word "tree," we access this idea by picturing a tree in our mind. The word itself isn't the actual tree; even the reproduction in our minds isn't the real tree.

We can even imagine this tree in our mind and sense or feel ourselves sitting against the tree. The mind is so powerful that we can manufacture an experience that doesn't exist. We can read a book about cosmic consciousness, understand the concept, and then imagine ourselves as one with the cosmos—floating everywhere, a drop in the cosmic ocean—and definitely feel this. But is it real? No. It's mentally and emotionally constructed.

Truth abides in the realm of existence. It's real. It isn't made up. It has an actuality and authenticity to it. The truth about something is the core of its verity. When we realize what isn't true about ourselves, the falseness vanishes. The untruth disappears. On the other hand, when we realize the truth of ourselves, the reality comes more into being—or, more accurately—into conscious awareness.

Truth has a consistency about it. Something that's true continues to be the way it is. There's an unchangeableness about it. When we say that something is true—like a true course—we mean it doesn't alter. It continues its path to the goal and doesn't veer off. There's an inevitability about it. It will always be there for us or for another. It's forever. It won't disappear. It won't fade. It continues to be itself no matter what we think about it.

We'll expand on the understanding of the nature of truth later in this book in the section on "direct experience." But first, I invite you to do the following exercise to get an idea of what I'm talking about. To begin, find a chair and sit on it.

THE CHAIR EXERCISE

First, notice what it is that you're sitting on. Be in the feeling of it. Take a few moments to settle into the experience of the chair.

Now, get the idea that a special friend spent many hours of labour making this chair for you. They made this out of great connection with and friendship for you. They invested hours and hours of loving work to make this for you. Really get into the belief. For a few minutes, imagine this and let it in... then note how you feel about the chair.

Shake this image off, and let that feeling go.

Now, get the idea that the colour of the chair is an unhealthy hue, and that science has verified that this particular colour emits toxic, carcinogenic radiation that seeps into your skin. Get the idea that a lot of research has been done on this, and the toxicity of this colour is a well-established fact. Really get into that belief. For a few minutes, imagine this and let it in... and then note how you feel about the chair.

Shake that off, and let it go.

Next, consider the idea that a very holy person—a spiritually advanced person whom you greatly admire—spent years and years meditating in this chair. They had many great spiritual realizations while sitting there. Really get into that belief. For a few minutes, imagine this and let it in... and then note how you feel about the chair.

Shake that off, and let that feeling go.

Then look at the chair again. Has it changed?

Is it different from what it was when you started the exercise?

I bet it's still the same chair as before the exercise.

Well, what changed during the exercise?

It was your belief or the way you thought things were. This changed your experience, right? The chair was still a chair all through the exercise. To an outside observer, it continued to be the same chair no matter what you thought about it.

So, the chair is like the truth: the way reality is... the way things actually are.

There's the fact of the chair just being a chair, and then there's our perception of it. Our experience of the chair is different from the chair itself. It's imposed on the chair. It depends on what we're thinking, not on the actuality of the chair. When we have a different view or belief about the chair, our experience of the chair changes even though the chair stays the same. It's our thoughts about the chair that change our experience of the chair, but, in reality, the actual chair continues to be the same even though we have different thoughts about it.

Just like the chair, truth is independent of our thinking. It isn't defined by our beliefs. It's separate from our concepts. It isn't the label or the name we attach to things. The idea of a mountain isn't the mountain. The name of anything is only the label that points to it.

We don't make the mistake of going into a restaurant and eating the menu thinking it's the food. The menu is just a description. Even our understanding and knowledge of a thing is still not the actual thing. We may extensively understand the chemical composition of a peach, be able to identify all its nutrients, and even comprehend the minute interactions that take place between the juices of the fruit and our taste buds, but this is still not the same as actually tasting the peach. Similarly, having an intellectual knowledge of love isn't the same as the wonderfully exhilarating feeling of being in love. Therefore, the only experience the mind has is of the thought of a thing, not the thing itself. Its only experience is theoretical and not reality.

Yet, so often on the spiritual path, we think an intellectual understanding of the concept of enlightenment, awakening, or spirituality is the actual thing. We listen to the guru explaining their understanding of existence, and the ideas all make sense, but the beliefs are all second-hand. Yet, we take them in as "truth."

We'd be repulsed by the idea of swallowing someone else's predigested meal, yet, so often, we swallow a guru's predigested belief system wholeheartedly without a gag, a burp, or a belch. Certain animals feed their young this way, and this is how they mature, but eventually they grow up and seek their own food. If we're to become self-sufficient in our spiritual development, surely we should move beyond this stage of spoon-fed infancy, beyond the deception that thought, concepts, names, ideas, labels, beliefs, doctrine, and all that hoopla is reality.

Let's grow up and move beyond this trap. Let's understand that thought isn't truth. Let's understand that truth isn't a product of the mind. Truth is independent of the mind. It's the pure and simple fact of the reality of something. It's the way things actually are.

> *"The heart of the matter is that we are living in a culture which has been hypnotized with symbols—words, numbers, measures, qualities and images—and we mistake them for, and prefer them to, physical reality. We believe that the proof of the pudding is in the chemical analysis, not in the eating."*
>
> — Alan Watts, *Does It Matter?*

So, if truth isn't thought, how can we come to know the truth?

Well, once again, it's so obvious that we miss it: Truth can only be experienced.

TRUTH AND EXPERIENCE

Consider the life of a young child. If we look at a child before the age of five, we notice that their mind isn't yet fully developed, yet their capacity to fully experience is there. Children that haven't been too traumatized are fully present and completely engaged in life.

They're "being themselves to fullness." When they encounter a new person or experience something for the first time, they approach this in an expanded state of openness, wonder, and excitement. When they're happy, they're fully happy, and when they're hurt, they fully express their emotions—and, if allowed, release the emotion until it's exhausted. They flow with life, taking it as it is and letting it go, with only the memory remaining and with no residual resistance or charge attached. Only later, as the child grows up, does the analyzing capacity of the mind come into being.

When that capacity arises, the mind—in its self-reflecting nature—starts to separate itself from the experience and begins to categorize and organize the experience by associating similar people, places, and things from the past. Over time, as the storehouse of memories and associations build up, the child can access this memory bank and reflect on past pleasant or unpleasant experiences to make beneficial choices in the future.

But the experience of reality must come first. If there's no experience, there's no material to draw on to organize. Therefore, there's no thought. So, in a way, the mind's purpose is analogous to the purpose of our digestive system—to assimilate, in a non-physical way, our perceptions of life. But the "food"—the experience—must come first. Just as we can't live on imaginary or already digested food, so, too, we can't exist just on thought, which is merely a processed experience.

As we contemplate this, what becomes clear is: our experience needs to be pure, unfiltered, and uninterrupted. This is where true fulfillment occurs. If we're sitting on the beach watching the sunset with a loved one, it's only satisfying to the degree that we let the whole experience in. We're being fully ourselves in the situation. We're taking in the occasion to its completeness. There's a pristine and pure quality without anything mixed in by our perceptions. We let the experience in, be with it, and let it go. "Let in, let be, and let go" is the mantra of experiencing.

Jesus said that if you're to enter the kingdom of heaven, you must be as a little child. When you meet an enlightened person, you get the sense of immense wisdom but also inspiring innocence. The enlightened interact with the world as it is. They see you in the divinity that you are. They've contacted reality and experienced its fullness without anything getting in the way. They see the truth—the way things actually are—and, as a result, they act in harmony with the reality of your essence.

If there's nothing standing in the way between reality and ourselves, our perceptions of self, life, and others is clear. The mind can take this complete experience and do its job of organizing it so we can make wise choices in the future. If our experience is incomplete and half-digested, the mind has limited material to organize for fuller living. Just as a jury can't decide guilt or innocence on incomplete evidence, so, too, we can't make wise choices based on incomplete or muddied experience.

This is the problem that most spiritual paths have been trying to tackle for centuries: how to free us from our sense of separation and help us to fully experience the divine gift of existence that is our personal life.

Through the ages, numerous spiritual techniques have been devised to meet this challenge. I've tested many of these techniques, and I've observed many other individuals as they attempted to apply them to their lives. In my experience, spiritual disciplines often fail to deliver the desired results—not because their techniques are ineffective or faulty but because they don't take into account what actually blocks us from fully experiencing reality in the first place.

For example, if an auto mechanic doesn't perform a complete diagnosis of a problem with your vehicle, he'll probably fail to correctly fix it. He may even end up trying to fix a "problem" that didn't exist and thereby create another problem. Similarly, if a spiritual tradition aimed at correcting a human condition fails to take into account a diagnosis of how that human condition arose, that tradition will ultimately fail to help people find liberation. In fact, it may even create further bondage.

So, we must investigate and come to an understanding of what blocks us from experiencing the truth or the way things actually are.

Once again, with great respect for your own wisdom and investigation, I'd like to offer an observation for you to consider: Two of the major roadblocks on the path of spiritual awakening are trauma and socialization.

Chapter 4

BARRIERS TO AWAKENING

TRAUMA—BEING OVERWHELMED

I define trauma as "an overwhelming experience that we were unable to fully get through or process given our ability at the time of the incident(s)." We all have trauma. There are simply different degrees of it. Trauma can come from any type of event. It can entail any degree of severity—from being physically abused, to witnessing a pet being run over, to living with a critical parent for 18 years, to a momentary angry glance from a teacher we admired. It can be a sudden event or an ongoing difficult situation. It could be the result of continual neglect or abandonment. It could be the result of an injury, a surgery, or the stress of moving from one culture to another.

The main characteristic is that it's overwhelming for us at the time. It results from our encountering a situation (usually, but not always, when we're young) in which we were confronted with an experience of something or someone too difficult to handle. We feared that if we totally let that event in, it would destroy us, so we blocked the part of the experience that was too much for us.

If there were others involved the event, we may have suppressed whatever communication we needed to have with them. Perhaps we lacked the verbal skills necessary to be understood or felt inhibited about speaking. This could have been the result of others denying our communication either by punishing us, ignoring us, or not being present. These uncompleted communications to others associated with the event(s) often carry an emotional charge—anger, fear, grief, guilt, anxiety, rage, sadness, or any other emotion that arose as we were immersed in the situation. These feelings were too difficult to communicate to the parent, friend, teacher, or abuser. It may not have been safe to express the truth of our feelings to these people. We may have known intuitively that they, too, were hurt and just couldn't hear our pain. It might have been too overwhelming, in turn, for them to receive our communication. We didn't know how to say, "That hurts," or "I need you to listen to me," or, "I'm a real person just like you," or "Understand me," or "I exist here," or, "I want you to love me." So, we resisted the experience and held back what we really needed to say.

If the event occurred in childhood, our normal open and expansive nature started to contract. We pulled back our full engagement with the world and froze. We did the only thing we could do at the time, the second-best thing—diminish our radiance and be other than who we really are.

To protect our self from the overwhelming experience, we decided to behave differently than our authentic self and to take on a particular belief about life, others, or our self. In so doing, we cemented our self into a set pattern of behaviour and fixed beliefs that we continually superimposed onto reality (just as we did in the chair exercise).

The result is that we withdrew partially from life and began to live more and more in our mind, in thought. Instead of openly engaging with life, the trauma caused us to recoil, freeze, become hyper-vigilant, and keep life at a safe distance. We were trying to figure life out first before living it.

This stuck state is what I call "the reactive mind." It's composed of all the overwhelming experiences, the incomplete communications to others, and the erroneous beliefs we've made up about self, life, and others and all the ensuing emotions, thoughts, and body sensations associated with these original experiences.

This stuck state is like a large battery. The battery is solid and substantial, yet it has an energetic charge. Likewise, it's as if we experience life plugged into a battery connected to an automatic switch. When we meet situations and people that are similar to the past overpowering event, the switch is triggered, and the energetic charge of our battery is released in inappropriate over- or under-reactivity, which causes us to create more havoc and negative karma in our lives.

BEN'S STORY

A good example of this is a client I worked with in a one-on-one session called Clearing. Ben grew up with a depressed and judgemental mother who was a survivor of a Jewish concentration camp in World War II. His mother never recovered from her experience and lived from the belief that life is only terrible suffering. Young Ben's joyful exuberance was too much for his mother, and she was frequently critical of his expressions of happiness or pleasure. His natural zest for life challenged her negative beliefs, and she reacted by coming down hard on him and telling him to stop being joyful. His response was to shut down his inherent happiness.

Ben didn't understand why his mother behaved the way she did toward him. He was too young to possess the verbal capacity to express what he was going through and tell his mother how her behaviour affected him, so all of these incomplete communications became stored in his memory. Because they were associated with feelings of great distress, he pushed them deep down into unconsciousness in order to distance himself from the pain.

As he grew and developed a personality, he incorporated these unconscious beliefs and feelings into his own self-identity, which was reinforced by self-blame. He concluded that his own being was at fault, not his mother's. He illogically decided that his mother's reactions to him were unloving because he was unlovable. As a result of this decision about his identity, he came up with a false solution: to only be good or nice or loving and to express only what was socially acceptable as an outer compensation for his perceived inner defect. These decisions resulted in a stuck state inhabited by sadness, fear of being himself, and self-anger. These traits manifested physically in Ben as a slight sensation of trembling in his chest, a heaviness in his forehead, and a slight queasiness in his stomach.

By taking on the point of view of being unlovable, Ben ended up perceiving himself through a lens that cast a dark colour of imperfection on all the bright spots of his being. And, despite his desperate attempts to prove his worth by acting in ways acceptable to his mother, he was unable to heal his inner sense of being unlovable or help his mother heal her inner wounds. Because "doing" is in a different universe than "being,"—which doesn't transform one's sense of identity—over time, his self-loathing increased.

Just like any human being, Ben made mistakes, but he was only able to recognize the behaviours that validated his "I'm unlovable" theme. He overlooked any actions that weren't consistent with this belief. Behind his outer presentation of "being nice," he sank deeper and deeper into self-dislike, and this perception came to be mirrored by others. He attracted people who criticized and mistreated him just as his mother had done in his earlier years. The emotional charge associated with all the uncompleted communications to his mother began to seep into his close relationships, and his over-reactivity resulted in relationships full of struggle and turmoil. He blamed others for treating him in uncaring ways, thus re-creating the victim/perpetrator game he had with his mother. Ben created the same story that he'd experienced in childhood. Although it featured different actors, it was the same drama.

Guilt and self-shaming set in. By mistreating others out of his unconscious reactivity, he continued to be mired in a negative cycle of guilt and shame that reinforced his sense of not being lovable. He'd say to himself, "I do bad things; therefore, I'm a bad person and I deserve to suffer." His life had become like his mother's: a crouched shadow living among crooked shadows.

Fortunately, in the work that Ben did with me in a form of therapy called "Clearing", he was able to go back to the origin of his "I'm unlovable" decision. He imagined his mother as being present in the session, completed his communications to her, and uncovered for himself the reality that he was born as a magnificent, divine being who'd become innocently trapped in an erroneous belief about himself. He realized that it was his mother's problem, not his. As the understanding dawned on him, instead of being angry at his mother, he developed love and compassion for her and treated her more tenderly whenever he was around her. He was free!

Ben's story illustrates something that's common to most of us. At some point in our lives, as a result of some kind of trauma, we withdrew from full involvement in life and began to see ourselves, life, and others through a tinted glass shell imprinted with our manufactured pictures of reality. From a distance, we inspected life, self, and others and expected them to all conform to our beliefs based on what we'd concluded from this past trauma. No matter which way we turned inside this shell, we gazed out at the world through these illusions.

It can be said that our experience of the world is intimately connected with the particular point of view that we've adopted. In this mental state, seeing isn't believing. It's more accurate to say that believing is seeing. We project our internal pictures onto reality, and that's what we see. The internal pictures are the composite meanings of everything we've made up and constructed around all the experiences we've had in our personal history. Even our senses are altered by the mind (as we saw in the chair exercise). We see what we believe, we take what we see to further confirm our beliefs, and we see more of that. It's an imprisoning cycle. The glass shell is our reactive mind, the buffer between self and reality, formed when reality is too hard to experience.

To summarize, the vicious circle of trauma is this:

1. Withholding: encountering an overwhelming experience, blocking a portion of that experience, and holding back communication to others associated with this experience.
2. Decisions: creating negative beliefs about self, life, or others that erroneously explain why the experience occurred.
3. State of being: feeling any number of emotions—such as sadness, fear, anger, shame, and guilt—as well as physical sensations in the body as a result of the decisions.
4. Actions/non-actions: reacting or suppressing behaviour or communicating or not communicating in ways consistent with our negative beliefs or decisions.
5. Predicaments: Re-creating, out of reactivity, situations similar to the original incident(s) that re-traumatize us.

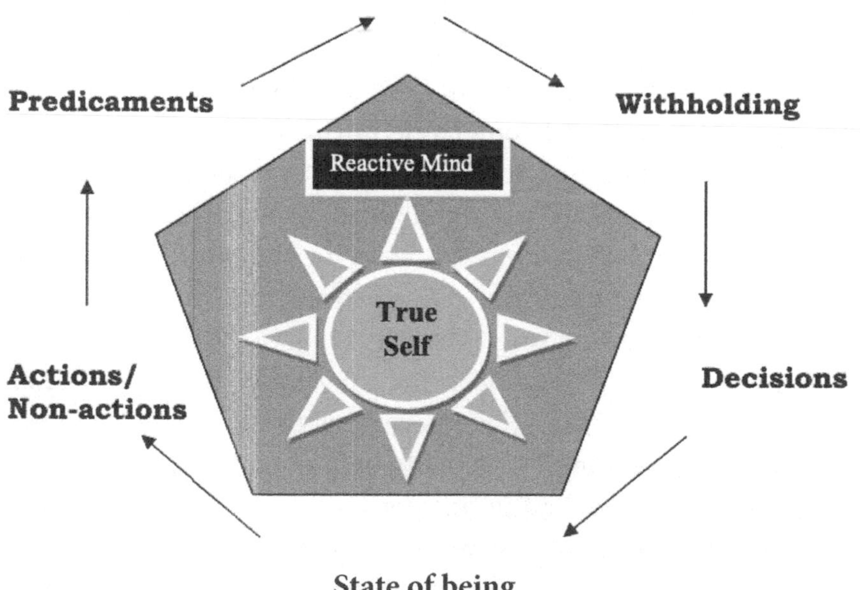

Since our awareness of truth is a function of our contact with reality, by spending more and more time in our minds or in beliefs about reality rather than in actual reality itself, we become more deluded and unhappy.

> *"Every time an external event reminds you of something in the past, you begin to experience the past... Your reactions are automatic, habitual, unconscious and pre-programmed. So, if you do not work through and bring it to a conclusion, it will continually repeat itself until it reaches a conclusion."*
>
> — Amrit Desai, *Voyage to Betterment*

SOCIALIZATION—MASS HYPNOSIS

Layered within these overwhelming experiences is our mass cultural environment: the sociological influences of our society, religious upbringing, peers, neighborhood, workplace, etc. Within these are a composite of many viewpoints, concepts, attitudes, and behaviour patterns that have caused us to see and interact with the world in pre-programmed ways. Most of these are unconsciously acquired. We're born as magnificent, pure, shining beings into the world; we're then shaped, molded, programmed, impressed, branded, or forced into being other than what we are, through the process of socialization. We lose touch with our true essence and learn very quickly that it's better to fit into another mold than fit with our selves.

Being socialized into a particular cultural environment is like being a novice actor on a stage with seasoned actors performing in an elaborate play. We must learn our lines and acquire our roles from others who've come from generations of actors before us. However, no one knows where the drama is leading. No one understands the purpose of the play. We all assume the older actors know, and very few of us are courageousness enough to break the illusion of the play and ask, "Why are we acting? What's this play all about?" We don't think to burst the bubble of make-believe and look behind the curtain or into the audience and find out what real life is all about.

In reality, we aren't prisoners of anyone in life. We're trapped in our minds by accepting the programming of how to see the world and ourselves. Through observation and training, we've concluded that others know the true way of living, and we imitate the behaviour and assumptions that inform how they see the world. We change ourselves like chameleons in order to be accepted and loved. We're the ones that haven't questioned this programming. We're totally unaware that we've done this to ourselves. Had we been placed, as young children, in a different culture, in a different family, or in a different country, we would have grown up acting differently with a markedly different perspective on life. But we'd still be trapped in our minds.

I once had a stark realization of this when I met a Chinese man who grew up in Jamaica. He had a Jamaican accent but was of Asian descent. In addition, he was a Zen Buddhist (a traditionally Japanese tradition), he played the sitar (an Indian tradition), and he was gay. He was a mixture of many different stereotypes, and I kept trying to pigeon-hole his behaviour into one of these. However, he didn't fit any of them. My mind was totally blown. The only thing I could do was to try to get to know him and relate to him as he actually was, which is the way we all want to be related to.

Major contributors to our socialization are the media and advertising. Advertisers spend millions of dollars of research money learning how to convince people through subtle manipulation to buy their products. It's estimated that people are exposed to an average of 40,000 commercials a year—2,800,000 over a lifetime. According to A.C. Neilson Co., every year, children are exposed to over 8,000 commercials for junk food and only 165 for healthy food. The effectiveness of this advertising is evident in the fact that there are now more overweight adults in the USA than normal-weight adults. Add to this picture the time we spend plugged into our I-pods and cell phones, and we begin to realize how little time we spend being in and interacting with the world the way it actually is.

In a sense, we live in a state of mass hypnosis. It's a misconception that we're only subject to hypnotic suggestion when we lose consciousness or fall asleep watching the hypnotist's pendulum. We're subject to suggestion any time we relax, get into a zoned-out state, or focus on something for an extended period of time. Does this not describe exactly what happens when we watch TV? We're mass programmed with hundreds of messages a day to not be our natural selves and to find our fulfillment outside ourselves in the thousands of consumer products advertised. Each one of these products eventually changes, degrades, gets damaged, decays, and ends up in the landfill. We're trapped in the temporary exhilaration of acquisition and the subsequent grief of loss. Our world is polluted with these illusions of consumer happiness as we overlook our real source of fulfillment: the connection to ourselves—a connection we lost as children. Therefore, we don't exist in a natural, authentic state of consciousness. Our everyday state of consciousness is actually an altered state attached to our erroneous expectations of the outer world. We're deluded into thinking that this state is normal, but normal only means a state of hypnosis shared by everyone else. Just because we share the same delusion doesn't mean it's real.

> *"If you do something enough times, the subconscious mind begins to believe that this behaviour pattern is what you want and therefore stores it for you and makes it part of your natural behaviour."*
>
> — Tom Nicholi, master hypnotist

Many years ago, I had an alarming and comical cosmic experience of the power of belief in creating a reality that didn't exist. It led me into contemplating the power of masses of people holding the same belief. The implications were illuminating and, at the same time, deeply disturbing.

THE TWITS OF SAINT TWINKLE

In the 1970s, I was living in a co-op house with some friends. We were pursuing a healthy, spiritual lifestyle and exploring all manner of New-Age practices and philosophies. There was an explosion of this across North America at the time. It seemed that everyone and his grandmother was coming up with some new belief system and healing modality. Just as a joke—and perhaps as a disguised cynical comment on all of this—one of the residents of the house, whose name was Ralph, and I decided to start our own religion. We called it "Twinklism."

We created a Saint of Twinklism called Saint Twinkle. Saint Twinkle was an animated, five-pointed star with two eyes, a nose, a smiley mouth, and seven rays of light emanating outward. We designated Saint Twinkle as the Patron Saint of Joy and Enlightenment. We were his disciples. We called ourselves the "Twits of Saint Twinkle," and we each fashioned a sacred garment to wear for worship, which was a large paper bag with eye-holes and a nose cut out. We drew a picture of our holy master on the bag just above the eye-holes (of course, where the third eye is located) and placed it on our head. We had a holy relic (a Beer Nut) and a sacred elixir (beer) that we had to drink before any ceremony with him/her (being New-Agey politically correct, the saint had no sexual orientation). Since this was going to be a secret society, we decided upon a secret greeting to indicate our membership. We'd extend our arms out toward each other, point our index fingers back at ourselves, and touch our fists together and say, "Who R U?" indicating our deep commitment to self-discovery. Since Saint Twinkle was the Saint of Joyousness and Enlightenment, the goal of the spiritual path was to open up our "Clown Chakra."

We'd put on our sacred garment—the paper bag—go into a darkened room, and light a candle. We'd start by meditating quietly in mock solemnity, and then just laugh whenever we felt like it. Of course, it was quite easy to laugh because what we were doing was so hilarious to begin with. We always felt good after drinking the sacred beer and paying homage to the holy Beer Nut and laughing ourselves half crazy.

We did this several times and decided—again, just as a joke—to present our new religion to the world. There was a protest rally against the Vietnam War, and we thought that since there were a lot of other philosophical societies and religious groups in the protest, we felt we needed a representation there as well. We put our sacred paper bags over our heads and walked in the parade, occasionally chanting, "Make bags not bombs, make bags not bombs." A few people asked us what we were doing, and we told them. Some people got the joke, but a lot of people thought we were nuts. We just pretended that *they* were crazy, and that we, of course, were of a much higher vibration than them, being the chosen ones of Saint Twinkle.

This hilarity continued for a few months and, at one point in a meditation, I decided that since channeling was finding its way into the New Age movement, I'd try my hand at channeling Saint Twinkle—once again, just as a joke. I'd go into a meditation after Ralph and I had chanted, "Ohm silly mahn, ohm silly mahn," and I'd communicate in a far-away, spaced-out tone some inane esoteric things about life on the seventh plane of some made-up, non-physical realm.

But, at some point, something changed, and I began to have a vague feeling that Saint Twinkle *was actually there*. I'd put my attention on him/her, feel the presence, and receive guidance. Remarkably, the guidance was quite cogent to my life. I began to feel the presence more often throughout the day as I went through my normal activities. Then, one day, something happened that changed everything.

I was traveling on the subway one morning and feeling very down about my life. I felt I was going nowhere, I wasn't getting what I wanted out of life, I was a loser—the whole, bummed-out thing. At one point, I had to close my eyes to hide my tears from the other passengers. Suddenly, a vision of Saint Twinkle appeared in my mind. The Saint was radiating light and appeared suspended right in front of me. He/she was mocking me with a profoundly sad face. The Saint's tongue was hanging down with an implied message: "Be happy. This is only temporary."

I was shocked at how clear the image and how palpable the vision was. I was also shocked at how something Ralph and I had made up became so real. I began to wonder about belief systems and religions. If just two of us were able to create something we could experience and communicate with, out of nothing—knowing full well it wasn't real from the start—what did that suggest about thousands or millions of so-called "believers?" Are they experiencing phenomena that are real, or is it simply a mass hallucination created by huge numbers of people putting their attention on the same thing? Or, did my friend and I create a false experience and then were subsequently contacted by an actual angelic being appearing as Saint Twinkle—a form we could accept? I don't know.

To this day, my experience of Saint Twinkle amazes and puzzles me. At the time, it was a major epiphany to realize the extent of the psychological forces that condition and imprison so many of us on the planet. I let go of the Saint Twinkle joke. The joke ended up being on us! But it helped me realize the double-edged sword of religious dogma. We aren't only the prisoner but also the jailer, imprisoned by our own device, limited by what doesn't exist. The insanity of it all was hilarious but also alarmingly painful. That backfiring joke changed my life!

It was then that I made it my life-long aspiration to experience the truth for myself, independent of any fabricated belief system. It's that commitment that still motivates me, years later, to assist and encourage others to go beyond belief to the truth itself and to not settle for anything less.

This whole story elicits several questions:

> If, as the result of our personal history—including our socialization—we aren't fully experiencing reality, how do we see what's true beyond our mental constructs?

> If our perceptions are limited and can be influenced by what we believe, how do we experience the universal truth that lies outside our mind?
>
> If (as we explored earlier) the spiritual path is all about living from the truth, how can we know the truth so we can live from it?
>
> And, finally, how does the spiritual teacher, spiritual master, or guru fit into the picture?

I've thought long and hard about these questions. In a sense, my whole life has been devoted to an examination of them. What I'm presenting here is a few suggestions for how you might start answering these questions The important thing is that you examine these questions for yourself. Let's look at some methods for going beyond belief to the truth itself and looking at the limitations of each of these, as we go along.

Chapter 5

MISTAKEN METHODS OF KNOWING ULTIMATE TRUTH

THE SCIENTIFIC METHOD

Measuring God

The universal scientific method involves five steps:

1. Formulating a question concerning a particular aspect of reality based on the knowledge already available to us.
2. Developing a hypothesis—using information that's already known or accepted—that predicts what will happen if we put our question to the test.
3. Constructing an experiment designed to test the hypothesis using observable data.
4. Analysing the empirical, or observed, data from the experiment to see if it confirms our hypothesis or not.
5. Communicating and discussing the results of our experiment and then constructing a theory verified by similar results repeated over time.

Through the scientific method, scientists have discovered many of the accepted truths of the physical world. The problem with the scientific method is that it's limited to the study of observable, objective data, which often comprises many independent, isolated events. Anything that's outside these events that could influence them may be overlooked.

Scientists are limited by the sensitivity of their measuring instruments and, although measuring devices can detect finer and finer gradations of physical reality—even to the subatomic level—they can't analyse the subjective components of a person's reality. Science has difficulty studying anything it can't calibrate. Quantum physics, which looks at the interaction between energy and matter, comes close, with many of its theories approximating the esoteric philosophy of ancient spiritual texts, but it's still not there yet. And, generally, Western science limits itself to the examination of objective, observable data that ignores the inner dimension of subjective experience. As such, science has its limitations.

AUTHORITY, TRADITION, CONSENSUS, AND APPEARANCE

What the herd heard is the word

Often people infer that authority figures know the truth because they have many students, or they're associated with an age-old lineage of an established practice and esoteric philosophy. Maybe there's a consensus among thousands of people that these teachers know the truth. Maybe the teacher looks and acts the part: long beard, white robe, and slow, hypnotic speech. However, they may simply be reiterating material they've been taught rather than speaking from their own experience. They may be teaching techniques that are harmful. (For example, I once heard of a guru who taught that the way to remove negative thoughts was to bang your head against a wall exactly 144 times. This may work—if for no other reason that it gives you a headache that distracts you from your negative self-talk!)

Modern history is littered with the debris of hundreds or thousands of followers of charismatic leaders who heard all the right things and believed the leaders knew the truth because everyone else thought they did. Authority, tradition, consensus, and appearance aren't proof that someone knows the truth—they're only proof that a lot of people believe they do!

INDIVIDUAL PERCEPTION

It's what I see, you see?

We perceive the objective world through our five senses. According to a commonly held belief, "seeing is believing." However, the information received through the senses is a second-hand experience of reality for the very reason that it's mediated by the senses. If the camera you're using to record the light patterns of a particular object has flaws in its internal structure, the image you record will have these flaws.

It's important to realize that several of our senses operate within a certain range of vibration. For instance, we can only hear the sounds that are within the human spectrum of hearing. Vibrations that occur above and below this range are imperceptible to us. Dogs and cats can hear sound frequencies outside the human range. Our ability to see colours is restricted to the range between infrared and ultraviolet. In addition, our depth or distance perception of sight and sound has limitations. Owls and eagles, for instance, can hear finer subtleties of sound at a greater distance than we can. So, we aren't getting the full complement of experience of reality and, therefore, aren't fully perceiving reality. If this is so, how can we be sure if we know the truth?

It's also important to understand that physical perception occurs by means of a complex set of intermediary events. It never occurs directly. For example, in visual perception, light energy enters the eye, travels through the lens, arrives at the retinal cells, and is translated into weak electrical charges that are relayed to the brain. All perception involves some kind of process, even before it reaches the brain. The brain then associates these electrical impressions with similar ones that are stored in memory, and we're able to recognize the visual input as a chair. These sensations all occur through a conduit of physical responses, memory accessing, and interpretation. Any break, disability, or malfunction in the system can produce an error. If there are problems with the retina, we can get a distorted image and not see the chair accurately, which can cause the brain to interpret it as something else. As far as mental perceptions are concerned, the chair exercise described earlier provides proof of the fact that we're capable of creating a sense of something real simply through the process of thought. This ability is under both conscious and unconscious control.

Individual perception is indirect. The sensation is here, and the self is over there. There's a separation between the perception and the perceiver, and a process bridges the gap. There's a pathway between the two, but there's no union. So, although there's a certain amount of reality that we can perceive with our senses, we have no guarantee that all of what we see, hear, touch, taste, and smell is accurate.

AFFIRMATION, POSITIVE THINKING, AND VISUALIZATION

Fake it 'til you make it, even though you make it fake

Teachings abound on the subject of positive affirmations. The general practice is to begin with a statement that a person wishes to be true about him- or herself or life and declare this repeatedly. Through the process of repetition, the person perceives a mental and emotional shift and feels more positive and energetic.

The shift is about moving thought around in the mind, emphasizing one type of thought to the exclusion of others, and creating a new perception—much like what Ralph and I did as the Twits of Saint Twinkle. We may affirm, "I'm a wonderful, radiant, light being," and there may be an element of truth to our affirmation. But what if it isn't true? If it isn't, we're just adding another delusion to our set of deluded beliefs.

Positive affirmations have a place in bolstering self-esteem and increasing a sense of positive orientation to the self, but they don't have a place in our goal of knowing the truth of who we are. We're just taking what we want to be true and, through a process of reinforcement, building an experience of ourselves that matches the way we want to feel. In fact, many spiritual teachers substitute positive affirmations for the truth. After years and years of stating the elements of a belief system over and over, students may begin to have spiritual experiences consistent with the dogma, but that doesn't mean they've discovered the truth itself. In addition, their experiences may become limited to the parameters of the dogma they're exposed to. If they do have a deeper realization, they may reject it. Oftentimes, the goal of the particular spiritual path—whether it's the experience of non-self, the void, non-duality, or cosmic consciousness—determines the kind of spiritual experiences people have.

LOGIC

Fundamentally mental

Logic is an intellectual process that consists of one or more premises and a conclusion. A premise is a statement offered in support of a claim that's being made. Premises and claims can be either true or false. In the process of logic, one presents an argument to prove something to be true or false. One begins with a statement or a premise that one knows is true and adds in other statements that are known to be true to arrive at a third statement or conclusion that's said to be logically deducible from the prior statements. For example, one can say that some philosophers are Platonists, and some mathematicians are philosophers; therefore, some mathematicians are Platonists. This is a sequence that comes to a logical conclusion. For logic to operate, one must be sure that the component statements are, in fact, true. If they're not, one can come to a false conclusion.

In many ways, logic limits its concern to the task of verifying a truth rather than discovering truth itself. It must first begin with premises that are already known to be true. For instance, I can say that science has proven that the physical universe is composed of energy. My body is part of the physical universe. Therefore, I am energy. This may seem like a logical statement and entirely valid. In fact, many spiritual seekers have made this erroneous conclusion. However, there's an assumption that my identity is physical or that who I am is physical.

As stated, the problem with logic is that it must start with premises that are known to be true. There are a limited number of concepts that we know are true, so our use of logic is necessarily limited to those concepts. As well, logic is limited to the intellect, and we've seen that the mind can only take the elements of experience it knows to be true and organize them. It can't know the ultimate truth because it doesn't have the ultimate experience within it as a premise to start with. Therefore, it can't prove or disprove anything related to ultimate truth.

> *"We may learn things by (1) hearsay or on authority: (2) by the mere suggestion of experience: (3) by reasoning; (4) or by immediate and complete perception... this last mode of knowing proceeds from an adequate knowing of the absolute nature of things."*
>
> — Benedict Spinoza from *Cosmic Conscious* by Maurice Buck

OCCULT AND PSYCHIC REVELATIONS

Inner sensing beyond the outer

Many people have had profound experiences of leaving the body and going into other realms, of hearing deceased loved ones or divine beings speak to them, of seeing visions of celestial worlds, of hearing an inner voice relaying impressions or intuitions about others and themselves, of feeling energetic releases, of viewing scenes of past lives, etc. These extraordinary occurrences happen to sensitive people frequently on the spiritual path and aren't unusual. Important insights can be gained from these experiences that can transform and inform our lives.

However, people can get trapped in wanting more and more of these experiences, thinking they represent a spiritual realm of ultimate truth. These experiences aren't to be discounted, but they should be differentiated from ultimate truth. They point to a finer, subtler realm than the physical world that's perceived not by the outer senses but by the inner senses of psychic seeing, hearing, touch, feeling, etc. These are much like the outer senses but are focused inward to a subtler space.

It's certainly important to cultivate our ability to "look within," but we should also realise that these inner senses can be deceiving, just as they can be accurate. This inner world is much more fluid and amorphous and, as such, is subject to interpretation. It takes more skill and considerable training for individuals to work within these realms to distinguish what's real from what's subject to the mind's influence. Although there's significant learning in these realms and great wisdom that can inform and uplift our lives, many spiritual seekers can get waylaid in this territory, thinking that the ultimate truth of self, life, and others is found here.

It's important to note that the process of "sensing" is operational here, with the same complex of intermediary events as with our physical senses. Just as our outer senses are subject to manipulation by our beliefs, so too are our inner ones. It's still in the realm of indirect experience.

DOGMA DOO-DOO

Somebody else's answers

We talked earlier about how thought is just a description of truth and that the mind can only experience thought and not reality.

Basically, dogma is somebody else's thoughts, packaged and organized into a set of concepts, theories, or stories. At best, dogma is supported by logic, but often it's not. We might say that dogma is a fixed set of second-hand beliefs promoted by a guru or teacher on a spiritual path that we believe is a first-hand description of reality. We accept it because the dogma appears to fill in all the empty holes in our understanding and appeases the discomfort of our "not knowing." It saves us from having to put in the effort to find the truth for ourselves. We might say it's the lazy way out. In many cases, dogma is based on someone's authentic mystical experience, so it comes with a sense of authority. Often, if the teacher is part of a tradition or lineage, the teacher's genuine spiritual experience may be mixed in with the dogma and communicated within the context, language, and jargon of the accepted teachings, so the mixture has a ring of validity. In the face of this seeming certainty, we willingly suspend our disbelief and take on the teacher's description (or menu) as reality (the food).

Even if the teacher is fully enlightened and is communicating the way reality actually is, this still has to be translated into language or a representation and can't be fully transmitted. A picture is still a picture. The map is not the territory. A model of reality, no matter how accurate in detail, is still a reasonable facsimile.

Over time, as the dogma is repeated, we become indoctrinated into believing that the teacher's first-hand experience is our first-hand experience. In fact, it's a belief system that's second-hand and could very well be third- or fourth- or 22nd- hand if the teacher is caught up in presenting the dogma that was passed down through his/her lineage.

> *"Filling the mind with all the highest spiritual teachings will not lead to liberation. Forget all you know, observe your experience and freedom will follow."*
>
> — Wayne Liquorman, *Eastern Mystics*

Many dogmatic spiritual paths are faith-based. We're persuaded to accept the point of view of existence on faith alone. We're extolled that we must first believe, have faith, have trust, set aside our doubts and confusion, and take on a predigested way of seeing life, God, love, ourselves, and others in order to know the truth. "Believe what is written first and then you will come to know." But we really don't come to know the truth through this path of faith. We only come to know what someone else says is the truth.

There's a certain value in accepting things on faith. Faith can create openness to new experience and counteracts an attitude of cynical disbelief. But faith often extends into blind faith, in which one goes to the extreme of becoming open to believing only what the authority figure says is true. As we become fully indoctrinated into the belief system, we may have some insights from time to time that seem like they're genuine, but, in reality, they're just like vowels in a *Scrabble* game. We move them around, up, and down to create different combinations of the dogma, but the basic elements are still all the same. There's a sense of novelty that comes from moving things around, but, in reality, there's nothing new.

THE DANGERS OF DOGMA

The danger of dogma is three-fold:

1. It limits the realm of our spiritual experience to the boundaries prescribed by the dogma.
2. It can create false experiences that appear to be real.
3. It opens us up to cult indoctrination and all the abuses of fundamentalism.

Limits of Dogma

Let's begin with the first danger. If we take on someone else's second-hand belief as our first-hand experience, it becomes a point of view, a way of seeing reality rather than an experience of reality. We use that point of view of the dogma as a reference point to measure and evaluate further ideas and experiences. These are rejected, manipulated, or reshaped by the mind to fit into the dogmatic framework.

The tragedy here is that a person can only go as far in their spiritual development as the dogma can take them, and then they'll cease to make progress. Once they get stuck, the only sense of progress they feel comes from the continual reinforcement of or addition to their dogma. But this is just rearranging and reconnecting the content of the mind and feeling some effects. Eventually, their spiritual path becomes dull and boring, and they need more dogma to feel a sense of newness.

Jill's self-deception

Jill, a woman who attended one of my retreats, was part of a belief system that strongly maintained that the self doesn't exist. At one point in the retreat, she began to enter into a divine experience in which she perceived not only divine love but also perceived herself as *being* divine love. As she began relating her direct experience, she started to radiate from that divine state. However, as soon as she recognized that her direct experience contradicted the dogma of her teacher, she backed away from her experience. She couldn't let go of the belief in the non-existence of self and, at the same time, be divine love. Her direct realization challenged the engrained structure of her dogma. For her to accept that direct experience, she'd have had to let go of that structure and disagree with her teacher. Instead, she chose the security of that structure rather than to dwell in her true nature. She fell out of union with her divine being. This was a tragedy for herself and for all others that she could have met in life who would have been touched by that radiance of love.

False Experience

The second aspect of a dogmatic approach is that we can easily create erroneous experiences out of dogma and believe them to be true, even though they were self-created. This is a common dynamic—well-known in the field of cognitive psychology—in which an individual who takes on a particular inner point of view about events will actually outwardly impose that point of view on those events and subsequently experience sensations and perceptions that are, in fact, inconsistent with the reality of those situations. (Remember our chair exercise?).

During my work at a retreat center years ago, I witnessed a spiritual teacher who taught a particular concept of human awakening and described in detail to his students all the feelings, characteristics, and perceptions he'd had in his cosmic experience. He then guided them through a meditation in which they were told they'd experience his same level of consciousness. Invariably, every student reported an experience that conformed exactly to his experiences. All the students were impressed by the great teachings and techniques of this master. However, it was clearly apparent that the experience they had was completely manufactured in their minds to conform to the teacher's belief system.

The trap here is that many spiritual seekers—out of faith in a dogma—can actually create or impose upon genuine spiritual experience phenomena that don't exist. They may then proceed in their lives thinking they've had divine illumination, and, when a genuine opportunity for direct spiritual experience comes along, they'll bypass it, thinking they've already achieved awakening when it was simply an illusion manufactured in their own mind.

FUNDAMENTALISM AND CULTS

The third pitfall in accepting dogma is the possibility of indoctrination into a cult, often resulting in sexual, physical, emotional, or monetary exploitation. Most spiritual practice expands our consciousness and opens us up mentally and emotionally. In that expanded state—where there's greater inner aliveness and heart presence—we can let go of our normal defenses and, can ignore our intuition that something isn't right. If we haven't worked through enough of our personal trauma issues, our personal boundaries may be weak, and we can become susceptible to manipulation from charismatic individuals. Often, individuals who get caught in a cult have a prior history of abusive relationships. They may be looking for the ideal father or mother in the spiritual leader. They may be looking to the spiritual community for a sense of family, familial love, and security that they never had as a child. When they find this in the leader and the spiritual family gathered around the leader, they'll do almost anything to keep it. Sadly, some spiritual leaders have a sociopathic or narcissistic personality and can exploit their students by making them feel special or more advanced than others or the rest of society. The sociological pressure within such a group to conform can be manipulated to the point where people will do almost anything to be in the dysfunctional "family."

It's important to be aware of the characteristics of a cult so you can recognize them and avoid such a group. To be forewarned is to be forearmed. Here are some common aspects of a cult:

1. Unquestioning adherence to a set ideology or philosophy as the ultimate truth, which must be taken on faith and not questioned.
2. Zealous admiration, subservience, and commitment to a self-appointed, "absolutely certain," charismatic leader who claims to have a special spiritual illumination or divine gift and demands loyalty (sometimes through several lifetimes) and dictates the behaviour of his/her members.
3. Exalted status of the group, the leader, and the ideology that claims they're the "only way" to the salvation of self or humanity.
4. Perception of the leader as perfect and unaccountable for his/her actions. Any actions that are reprehensible are considered as above reproach or as some divine teaching lessons for the person or group. Any criticism of the leader is turned back on the students as "projections" of their own lack of higher consciousness.
5. Justification of any unethical or immoral means as a necessary end to promote the advancement of the group and its bogus goal to uplift humanity.

6. Heavy coercion and pressure to devote excessive time, money, and effort to group activities, especially fund-raising and the recruiting of new members to the point where people ignore their inner voice and engage in activities they normally wouldn't.
7. Control and manipulation of members through shame, group dynamics, hypnotic techniques, alienation, sleep deprivation, over-work, shunning, etc.
8. Use of special language, dress, symbols, jargon, etc., which have a special meaning only to those within the group.
9. A belief and fear that the world outside the group is somehow dangerous and tainted and that the only way to salvation is to be separate from the world or socialize only with group members.
10. Drone-like behaviour of group members who behave, dress, and speak the same.

Not all the criteria need to be met to indicate the existence of a cult. One or two of these may be sufficient. It's an interesting exercise to use the above characteristics of a cult to scrutinize any existing group, organization, religion, political party, business, or even country. If we did this, we'd be amazed to find major or minor cults everywhere.

Think of the Al Qaeda in Afghanistan, the Spanish Inquisition, the Confederate States, and Nazi Germany, just to name a few. What was the basis of all these cults? Indoctrination into a dogma! The dogma of the superior Aryan race; the dogma that Jews are evil and need to be destroyed; the dogma that women who used herbs to heal in the Middle Ages were witches; the dogma that men and women of a different colour than those in the cult are inferior and therefore can be enslaved; the dogma that if I carry a bomb and explode it in a crowded marketplace, I'll go to heaven; the dogma that it's okay to lie about weapons of mass destruction to invade a country under the guise of bringing democracy there; the dogma that the end always justifies the means. How many wars have been caused by dogma, where one country—often in the name of God—fights another that also has God on their side? The pattern repeats itself throughout the ages. It seems that it's brand-new history, same old news. Everyone has God standing up for them! Why won't the real God just sit down!

The Tragedy of Dogma

The tragedy is that we don't kill one another out of the truth; we kill one another out of a facsimile of truth—a shadow, a chimera, lies, or something that doesn't exist. We destroy one another for nothing. This is insane. This is beyond tragedy. If we let the insanity of all of this in, it would shatter us. We'd fall to the floor and cry out in despair. We'd yell out to the world in a rage in the hope of shattering the ice around all the hearts of those who've destroyed their neighbors because they held different beliefs. The differences were only in their minds, not their hearts. If we could sit down and have tea across the table from the "enemy" that we've been socialized to believe is evil and ask them what their life is like, we'd discover "common folk" like us. We'd discover someone who wants a good life for their family, who wants to contribute to the world, who wants to love and be loved. To realize the destructive power of political, religious, and economic dogma to create suffering is shocking. Even more shocking is this: if we use the definition of dogma as "a set of second-hand beliefs" and honestly examine how much of what we believe is actually second-hand and how much is our first-hand knowledge, we'd be dumbfounded. We'd recognize we know extraordinarily little about reality. We'd realize that what we don't know is a whole lot more than what we do know.

So why on earth do we settle for dogma and belief in something that we don't know is true when there's so much of reality out there that we're unaware of and can try to know? We settle for faded fables when the shining truth is just behind the curtain of all the concepts, names, and labels we give to things.

To come to these realizations—as demoralizing and deflating to our mind as they are—is an important epiphany on the spiritual path.

To see the destruction that dogma has created can break our hearts, but maybe our hearts need to be broken…broken open. With these understandings, we can find a renewed desire to let in any experience that comes along in life, as it potentiality could contain the seeds of awakening, while those caught in dogma only consider that which confirms a pre-set belief system.

There's a saying that "if you want your life to change, you have to give something up." I'd like to suggest that one of the things we should continually learn to recognize and give up, is dogma. The best place to start is inside our heads. It isn't only a great service to ourselves, it's the best gift to the world.

> *"We must approach life as though stepping from a dark chamber into a lighted one for the first time, without anticipation or expectation as to what we are to see or hear and then subject each experience to our own analysis, not coloured with the analysis of others. The person who really wishes to approach the mystical life in a frank manner… must not be a coward. He must not hesitate to oppose or challenge tradition"*
>
> — Ralph M Lewis. *The Sanctuary of Self.*

DOGMA-FREE ZONE

I think we should all have a dogma-free zone

Somewhere in our world

A place:

Where we can think our own thoughts and listen to our own voice.

Where all beliefs are considered as assumptions until we can directly experience them for ourselves.

Where "truth" isn't considered a four-letter word.

A guru-free zone:

Where we can bow down to ourselves and honour our own wisdom.

Where Buddhists can grow their hair really long and all Christians, Hindus, Jews, and Sikhs can hang-up their sacred hats before they enter (and, when they leave, will put on someone else's hat).

A place where fundamentalists, if they enter, will explode from their own inner bombast.

A spiritual, name-free zone

where we can pretend we're Popeye and say

"*I yam what I yam*" and totally accept ourselves.

Where we can look in the mirror without fear and see total magnificence.

A place where, when everything seems to be falling apart, we can let go

and let it fall into place.

Where we can be okay about not knowing anything

and allow ourselves to experience everything…

exactly the way it is.

That would be a great place.

I think we all should start by writing "Dogma-free zone" on a sticker,

slap it on our forehead, and look at each other…

Then laugh our heads off!

— Russell Scott, July 2008

Chapter 6

PERSONAL REALITY AND ULTIMATE TRUTH

INSIGHT

Personal Reality

We've all experienced insight. It's that flash of knowingness that often accompanies the concentrated contemplation of a problem. It can appear out of nowhere, often when we're no longer directly contemplating the problem. It's often accompanied by feelings of relief or delight. It can offer solutions to creative projects, personal dilemmas, or business endeavours previously not thought of. These epiphanies can run the gamut from how to rearrange the furniture in a room to the solution of a complex problem in physics. Insight can't be forced to happen and, although there are processes we can employ to improve the probability it will occur, nothing can guarantee its appearance. As Einstein once said, "The intellect has little to do with the road to discovery. There comes a leap in consciousness, call it intuition or what you will, and the solution comes to you and you don't know where, how or why."

Generally, insight occurs when intense focus on a problem or question is followed by a period of letting go of thinking about the problem—that is, active concentration is followed by passive receptivity.

Edison and Einstein commonly followed this procedure to arrive at their inspirations. Sometimes, insights can occur by contemplating one side of a choice and then the opposite repeatedly to produce a solution that's a combination of the two—i.e., thesis, antithesis, and synthesis. Another way to facilitate insight is the process of bissociation in which two elements or items not normally associated with one another are connected to produce an unexpected third element. This is often the method behind comedy. I once saw a comedian from Newfoundland do the famous, "To be or not to be, that is the question" speech from *Hamlet* in "Newfie jargon": "Ya either is er yer isn't, I figrs." Another method is to repeatedly expand and then contract the problem by contrasting full communication with summaries so that previously unclear elements of the problem are revealed and then restated until the problem is fully understood. The solution is often hidden in the problem, so a fuller understanding of the problem can often result in a solution insight. (See the exercise on Problem Solving for this technique.)

Even with these methods, there still isn't a direct link between where we start and where we end up. There isn't a conduit or process that contributes to the insight as there is with sensation or a connection among all the elements in the process as is the case with logic. There's no "via" or "by way of." The insight is spontaneous, and it's often accompanied by a sense of exhilaration when the tension between the problem and solution dissolve or laughter occurs at the obviousness of the solution. A common element of insight is the certainty of its reality or its appropriateness to the situation.

There are many theories about how this phenomenon occurs. One theory is that our inner consciousness is continually mulling over the various permutations of a problem, combing through many combinations of the elements of a situation as we go through our daily life. Another unusual idea is that spiritual beings psychically present a solution to us after investigating the entire set of options from a much more expanded viewpoint. Others who are more materialistically inclined suggest that it's just a neurological event much like a computer sorting through and comparing probabilities and arriving at the best possible solution.

Whatever the explanation, we often don't know how we arrive at the solution. It just appears. We know the idea is right and true even though there may not be logical proof. If asked how we know it's right, we'd just say that we know. There's an inherent feeling of validity.

Personal Insight and Spiritual Awakening

It's important, however, to distinguish between personal insight and spiritual experience. Insight is most often related to our personal reality or our personal situation in life. For instance, we may have an important understanding of how our behaviour originated in childhood or how to best use our body to swing a bat to hit a home run. These ideas will be true for us but may not be true for others. The mistake is that we may think that what's personally true for us is also true for others.

Some spiritual teachers make the same error. A guru may think that in his/her tradition, a particular meditation practice is always good for everyone when, in fact, other forms of meditation may be more suited to a person's disposition. A more nervous, physically active person may find walking meditation more beneficial, whereas an introverted person might do better with sitting meditation. We shouldn't make the mistake of assuming that our personal preferences—such as the clothes we wear, our habits of communication, our goals in life, or our individual values—should be the preferences of everyone else. We should understand this is just the truth, or the way it is, for us.

On the other hand, we should also know that just because we have a personal reality doesn't mean that there isn't a universal reality that applies to everyone. This can also be another error on the spiritual path—believing there's no such thing as a universal truth. It's easy to assume this, especially after going through the former list of all the ways we're limited in our perception of the truth. Since all the processes that we normally use to try to know the truth can't get us there, we may be tempted to conclude that there's no way we can know the truth, or there's no universal truth to be known. This is a recipe for cynicism and despair at the possible meaninglessness of life.

The good news is that universal truth *can* be known, and there's a way we can discover that truth for ourselves. This idea, this path, may be new to us. It's a revolutionary path that involves a new form of consciousness. It's called "direct experience."

DIRECT EXPERIENCE

The True Nature of Self, Life, and Others

This form of consciousness—direct experience—has been called by many names throughout the ages. A few of these labels are "awakening," "enlightenment," "illumination," "transcendence," "self-realization," "*kensho*" in Zen, "*anubhava*" in Hinduism, and "unitive consciousness" in modern psychology. It's often described as a life-altering spiritual experience in which one suddenly breaks through one's normal mode of sensing to become cognizant of the true reality of existence. It's also accompanied by a deep sense of peace, serenity, bliss, and inner harmony. Because it results in an exalted awareness of self, it's always life-altering.

Direct experience is often described in terms of what it's not. Like an insight, it's not accessed through a "via" or a process such as sensing or logic. It's also not accomplished through affirmations, visualization, positive thinking, or believing. As was illustrated earlier, we can easily manufacture an exalted sense of self through a process of repeating an affirmation or visualizing a scene of being at one with the universe, but this experience will fade without continual reinforcement.

Direct experience differs from insight in that it's much deeper. With insight, we're "in sight" of something. We're on the outside of a problem or issue and looking inside to see the essence of the phenomenon. With direct experience, we're in union with the thing we inquire into. We enter into it with our full consciousness. There's no duality between the perceiver and the perception. For a brief moment in time, we're no longer separated from our real essence. We've merged. We're one with ourselves or with life.

Direct experience is often described as a spontaneous event, a profound "aha" moment, a deep intuitive flash that lights up one's being. Suddenly, we know who we are, but this occurs in a way that's much more enveloping than an insight. It encompasses one's body, mind, and emotions—one's whole being. With it, there's a universal understanding or knowingness of the fact or the truth of one's existence. We're united with our true nature in such a way that we're not only experiencing the magnificence of who we are, but we know with absolute certainty the fact of our being.

Here's an account of an awakening experience from a participant in a retreat called the Enlightenment Intensive:

> *"Suddenly, I knew who I was. Tears just streamed down my face; I was so overwhelmed. It was so simple...and I was so grateful, not just for what I discovered about myself, but also for the total certainty associated with that experience. There can never be any doubt... I knew it in a way that didn't depend on any feeling, idea, belief or anything—I was just directly conscious of who I was."*
>
> — P.C., academic

The Spontaneous Event of Awakening

Awakening doesn't happen through a process. It defies understanding because it's a paradox. It's a way that has no way. It's an experience that initially isn't an experience, and then it becomes an experience. It's a knowingness that's beyond thought, but we try to feebly describe it through thought.

To be more specific, in direct experience, there are three spontaneous events that occur: union, knowingness, and experience.

1. **Union:** Our consciousness spontaneously fuses with the essence of our true self, life, or other individuals for a timeless instant. Some people describe this union as being like an implosion: all the separate parts of ourselves become one. The separation between the observer and the observed disappears.
2. **Knowingness:** We become suddenly conscious of that with which we've united. Without any procedure or method for arriving at this understanding, we know the essence of it absolutely. It's a complete understanding, an illumination or an influx of knowledge that transcends and far surpasses that which is ordinarily experienced or communicated by us.
3. **Experience:** As we fall out of the unity or implosion into truth, we now explode into the experience of ourselves, life, or another from the new vantage point. There's a new awareness that wasn't there before. It's like going into a darkened room and turning on the light. When the room was dark, we could see nothing, but, with the light on, we see everything. We've become en-light-ened about the room, becoming conscious of what was always there but we weren't able to see. For instance, if we suddenly fall into the knowledge that we're divine love or pure, absolute potential, we move into the exhilarating experience of that. There's an energy release, and our presence begins to radiate almost as if there's a light within us. People's experiences can range from extreme bliss and joy to a grounded sense of peaceful calmness as they come home to themselves.

It should be noted if all three of these events aren't present, the experience isn't one of awakening. We can be deeply in touch with ourselves in deep meditation and feel calm, blissful, and serenely at peace, but if we can't articulate who it is that's calm, it's not awakening. Conversely, we may be able to intellectually state an idea of self, but if we aren't in union with ourselves and in experiential self-connection, it's also not awakening.

Awakening is much like waking up, but waking up in a unique way. We suddenly become consciously connected to who we really are and the change is noticeable by others. There's an obvious change, but we don't change into something else. Actually, what happens is, we drop the personality with which we've been identified and fall into our true authentic self, becoming more able to present ourselves from this radiant state. The egotistical endeavour of trying to be someone else drops away. What we become is ourselves, not someone else. We allow who we've always been, but weren't previously conscious of, to "show up." The effortless simplicity of just being is uniquely satisfying, exhilarating, and revitalizing. It's like finally coming home to ourselves after years and years of being lost.

> *"The Ultimate is not something you attain; it is something you merge with. It is something you become."*
>
> — Sadguru Vasudeva, Eastern Wisdom

With awakening come tremendous benefits: inner peace, self-acceptance, fuller authenticity, inner certainty, the ability to connect deeply with self and others, enhanced meaning and purpose, and a deeper capacity for happiness and joy. Because one's life is based on a solid foundation of immutable truth, there naturally arises a greater strength to face any experience in life and persist through difficult times.

We realize that ultimate truth is knowable, and it's already in us, because, in reality, we are it. We are the truth itself.

ASPECTS OF DIRECT EXPERIENCE

Obvious Simplicity: Spiritual literature is full of accounts of spiritual seekers having enlightenment experiences and then laughing uproariously. This is because self, life, and others become completely obvious and naked, no longer in hiding. We laugh because we've been so diligently and desperately seeking, and, suddenly, the truth is revealed as plain as the nose on our face. We haven't seen it because the mind was so full of ideas, beliefs, prior experiences, and concepts that were projected onto our view of reality. It's as if we were wearing rose-coloured glasses and concluding that everything has a red tint. When we take off the glasses, the world now seems brand new. It really isn't any different; we're just seeing clearly for the first time. When we live from this pristine quality of perception, we tend to be more content with the ordinary, realizing there's no other place to go in life. We understand that everything we need to be happy is here and now. The greatest fulfillment is found in the present moment

> *"I yam what I yam, yuk, yuk, yuk, yuk, yuk!"*
>
> — Popeye

Permanence: For something to be true, it needs to be that way all the time. If it changes, it isn't true. For example, true love isn't true if, at some point, the person doesn't feel that love anymore. True love means: "I'll love you 'til I die." When we realize the truth of self, we perceive the God-self that's always been us and will continue to be us in spite of the changes in our bodies, personalities, careers, and relationships. This realization brings an inner strength and security. We know that no matter what happens to us, we won't be destroyed. We'll still exist. The fear of not existing or of dying is behind most of the fears that defeat us in life. With the realization of the immutability of the true self, we can face and overcome life's greatest challenges.

> *"Ultimate experience gives ultimate knowledge which casts out the ultimate fear, the fear of death."*
>
> — Ram Dass

Universality: When we perceive the true nature of life, others, and self, we understand that it's this way for everyone. It's the foundation of all philosophy and religion. After a direct experience, we can understand the deeper meaning of spiritual texts and spiritual writings. We understand that the divine dwells in all beings and all things, and we have more compassion for our fellow humans. We feel a greater connection to the mystery of life and feel at home in it. We feel a greater reverence for the planet on which we live and the universe in which we dwell.

Fact: Direct experience isn't dependent on acceptance or non-acceptance. It doesn't care whether we like it or not. It isn't subject to us admiring it. It simply is as it is. The truth exists independent of our awareness of it. Even if we aren't aware of it, it's still there. It isn't dependent on anything for its existence. No matter how much we affirm it or deny it or curse it or bless it or proselytize or condemn it, it will still be. It's an undeniable fact. There's an inherent authority about it. What's experienced is never diminished by doubt of its authenticity. There's always an inner conviction. Direct experience doesn't require re-inforcement by faith, belief, or affirmation. We always know the divine truth, even though we may fall out of the experience of it.

> *"Once one has seen the elephant, it is no longer necessary to accept on faith that the elephant exists."*
>
> — Early Zen saying (Soto school)

Reality: In fact, truth is the *only* thing in life that's real. Falsehood doesn't exist. It must be invented. And, in the face of truth, falsehood doesn't stand a chance, because the truth is the only thing that's real. When illusion stares the truth in the eyes, it vanishes into the dream from which it arose. So, when we experience the actuality of self and life, our sense of self-rejection diminishes. Others' opinions about us matter less. We're who we are, and life is what it is, no matter what others or we believe. There's a certainty and unpretentiousness that enters our lives. The tendency to try to be like someone else is lessened as we begin the new task in life of living in our authentic presence, presenting ourselves as we really are. Falsehood requires a lot of effort to be maintained, remain consistent, and be promoted.

When we experience the actuality of self and life, we experience a release of the life energy that's been required to prop up a false self. This vitality becomes available to move through the body and create greater health and psychological wholeness. Those who've awakened have a radiance about them. It's this authenticity that others really want from us in all our relationships. This authenticity is the result of being with reality as it is, even though when we enter the direct experience, it appears as if we have transcended reality or entered a state that exists in an outside, alternate dimension. In fact, we have, for a brief period of time, broken through the grip of the everyday illusion in which we existed and entered into true existence. What we directly experience in awakening is actually normal reality. We haven't transcended at all. The whole idea of transcendence is an error.

Ineffability: The awakening experience is difficult to communicate because it's beyond words or concepts or beliefs. Any experience, whether direct or indirect, loses something in the explanation. How can we get across the totality of the experience of eating a peach? The sensation of taste can't fully be converted into words.

The situation is even more problematic with a direct experience. Enlightenment is a shock to the mind. It surprises the ego because it's beyond its domain, beyond its governorship, and outside its kingdom. The mind grapples with trying to force it to fit into the landscape it's fashioned, but it can't. Sometimes the mind will try to deny the experience because it doesn't conform to the picture it's made up of the self, life, or others. If it's successful in this denial, the experience will become a memory, but it isn't truly gone. It's just been covered up and, years later, at the right time, it will surface in all its glory. Because of this inability of the mind to explain the knowingness, many spiritual traditions advise students to not do anything with the direct experience and avoid communicating it. This is a big mistake. The mind needs to make sense of it—to digest it as it were—to correlate prior experiences and confined concepts with the new experience and, in so doing, expand beyond our limited understanding of reality. This is best done by externalizing the experience through communicating it to a receptive person. Doing so helps to integrate the awakening and bring it into a more embodied form. It's for this reason that authors write and teachers teach, since the act of communicating helps them access more of what they know and solidify their understanding so it's more livable.

Liberating: Jesus once said, *"Know ye the truth and the truth shall set you free."* When we come to know the essence of self, we're released from the imprisonment of an illusion we've believed and dramatized for many years that's caused much suffering. With awakening comes a release of energy that's the result of letting go of the effort it takes to keep positive and negative beliefs in place. It takes a lot of internal psychic energy to hold onto these beliefs. When we realize the truth, we can let go of the need to hold onto these beliefs because no amount of believing or disbelieving can change what is. The truth isn't dependent on anything for its existence. A dog doesn't need to affirm that it's a dog in order to be a dog. That effort isn't required. But if the dog didn't know what it was and thought it was supposed to be a cat, it would need constant energy to maintain resistance to its true nature and its belief in being a cat. I've witnessed many individuals who've carried around significant pain in their lives as the result of a decision they made about themselves due to an early childhood trauma. When they revisited that decision and understood they could make another choice (e.g., that they weren't to blame for what happened to them as a child), the years of pain that had tormented them dissolved right before their eyes. They became freer to act from the true individual they actually are. I find it absolutely amazing to witness when this happens.

> *"As we awaken, we discover that we are not limited by who we think we are. All the stories we tell ourselves – the judgments,*

> *the problems, the whole identity of the small self, and the body of fear – can be released in a moment, and a timeless sense of grace and liberation can open for us."*
>
> — Jack Kornfield

There's a great power in knowing the truth. We don't have to believe what we already know. We just accept it. We don't have to prop up, justify, defend, or proselytize what we know. All that neurotic force is dropped, and we come home to a deeper discovery: the source of true happiness—which we've been socialized to believe by our modern media is outside of us—is already within us.

It arises naturally as a result of just being as we are. We don't have to do anything or have anything. Happiness is inherent in our being. The neurotic addiction to finding happiness outside fades, and the more we stay in touch with our true nature, true peace of mind arises. We realize that life is fulfilling to the extent that we're being ourselves in whatever experience we have. There's a permanent sense to the self and, as result, the fear of experiencing life begins to vanish. We're less distant from life and others, and life is lived more deeply and profoundly. Consequently, we have a greater willingness to experience life and process life experiences. We can access the wisdom that's naturally there in our world.

> *"When you know who you truly are, there is an abiding alive sense of peace. You could call it joy because that's what joy is: vibrantly alive peace. It is the joy of knowing yourself as the very life essence before life takes on form. That is the joy of Being, of being who you truly are."*
>
> — Eckhart Tolle

I realize that much of what I've presented in this chapter is intellectual, and I might be subjecting you to the same trap of trying to transmit the essence of a direct experience in words—which is one of the things I've been warning you that the intellect can't do. So, I'd like to relate an account of an enlightenment experience that a participant had during an Enlightenment Intensive, one of the retreats I facilitate. Compare this to the enlightenment of one of literature's great figures, Alfred Lord Tennyson. Feel into the experiences, and see if you can get a sense of the power and profoundness of the nature of direct experience:

> *"It was as if everything was connected, connected to me. All smells, all sounds, all sights, all things sensory seemed to be totally happening in me or me in them. There was simply no separation between me and light, me and sound, me and fragrance, me and other-than-me. I couldn't tell if I was hearing the sound in my head or where the noise originated. It was as if the image I saw was both in me, of me, as me. Isolation, separation, feeling alone or closed was absolutely not the case.*
>
> *I understood in that timeless moment all the teachings of the great ones—Jesus, Gandhi, Martin Luther King, Lao Tzu. I knew everything. I was living in the Tao. I was all things, all time. I was absolutely everything and nothing at all in the same moment."*
>
> — Stephen Garrett, Langley, BC,
> Enlightenment Intensive participant

> *"All at once, as it were, out of the intensity of the consciousness of individuality, the individuality seemed to dissolve and fade away into boundless being and this not a confused state, but the clearest of the clearest, the surest of the surest…utterly beyond words, where death was an almost laughable impossibility, the loss of personality but the only true life."*
>
> — Alfred Tennyson in *Cosmic Consciousness*
> by Maurice Buck

Chapter 7

ENLIFENMENT

AFTER AWAKENING

You may have heard the phrase, "Before enlightenment, chop wood, carry water. After enlightenment, chop wood, carry water." This is true. We go back to our life, where all the normal activities of life remain. As I said at the beginning of this book, *On the outside, we look like everybody else. We talk, walk, eat, sleep, work, relax, earn money, pay bills, wake, dream...* Yet, on the inside, we're different. After awakening, we're awake to the divinity of life, others, and ourselves. We now see others and life from a new and truer vantage point. We have a more intimate relationship with ourselves within all the same endeavours of life that we had before our direct experience. We've been to the mountaintop, tasted truth, seen divinity, and experienced a more expansive vista of reality. In many ways, it's like a rebirth. There's first our physical birth. We're born into a body, but, over time, with trauma and socialization, we lose the connection with our true self. If we're lucky, at some time later in life, we're reborn into our spiritual self by awakening to our essential nature.

Many spiritual traditions consider awakening to be the end of the spiritual path, primarily because, in most traditions, it takes so long—a lifetime or more—to get there! But now there are modern methods that can take us there in a fraction of the time. (See the chapter on the Enlightenment Intensive). It's a paradox. Awakening is the end of the path… and it's not. It's the end in the sense that we stop searching for self. When we "answer" the question of "Who am I?" that's the end of the project. It's a done deal. We know for certain who we are. To continue to ask the question is fruitless and often exasperating. Asking it is as useless as asking, "How do I get to the supermarket" when we're already there. But there's more to the spiritual path than just awakening.

"True-Self-Actualization" – *Be You to Fullness*

When the problem of "not knowing the self" is resolved, a new problem arises: the project of how to live from this awakened state. In some circles, this can be called self-actualization, but I prefer to be more specific. The terms "true-self-actualization" or "enlifenment" are more descriptive. It's the process of cultivating and living from our new awareness once self-realization has occurred. In other words, it isn't enough to have an enlightenment experience; we must work toward what we might call "steady being—the state of being in touch with our true self and consistently relating to others from our essential nature rather than through our personality or reactivity from past trauma. enlifenment or true-self-actualization means moving from self-realization or an enlightenment experience to full enlightenment. Although there are many definitions for someone who's fully enlightened depending on the spiritual tradition, it generally refers to someone who's fully dissolved the reactive mind so they're no longer stimulated by and over or under reacting to present circumstances because of past trauma. They're surrendered to life with no tendency to resist or grasp onto pleasant or painful experiences; i.e., they respond to life and others in a way appropriate to the situation, and they're in constant relationship with the universal self and radiating wisdom, peace, and compassion. Let me share a couple of examples.

Cultivating the Awakening Experience

Ramana Maharshi, one of India's greatest sages, while inquiring into the question, "Who am I?" had a profound enlightenment experience at a young age. It's reported that he spent the next 10 to 20 years deepening and integrating his self-realization until he reached full enlightenment. It's also reported that after the Buddha had his "big bang" enlightenment experience, he spent many months continuing to sit in meditation. What were they doing? My theory is, they spent this time putting their attention on their true self and letting the initial enlightenment grow, mature, and ripen.

Let me explain it this way. In many ways, the possibility of awakening is like a seed that dwells latently within us. Who we actually are is always there, but we just don't notice this. However, when we water it with spiritual practice, at some unpredictable moment, that seed will burst open with new life—which is akin to the bursting forth of the new awareness of directly experiencing existence. This is the new life, the new birth, that I've talked about, but for that seed of awakening to grow, it needs to continue to be tended with sunlight, watering, nourishment, and weeding. How do we do this?

Let's look again at the Buddha's experience. My theory is that he stopped the technique he was using to become enlightened because it was no longer necessary. He was now in union with the divine itself and, as a result, he simply abided in it. Another way of saying this is: he focused his attention on his new knowingness as his meditation practice and let go of the technique that led him to enlightenment because he didn't need it anymore. In so doing, his awakening and knowingness continued to expand. There's a universal principle that whatever we put our continued attention on comes more into existence. We have many New-Age philosophies—from *The Secret* to the *Law of Attraction*—that have reintroduced this principle from many age-old mystical traditions. In accordance with this principle, he was putting the (sun)light of his attention on his true, enlightened essence and, as a result, brought the connection to his real self more into fullness.

So, after enlightenment, we need to spend a good amount of time letting go of the technique that got us enlightened and place our attention on the fruit or the truth that we realized in order to ripen and stabilize that experience.

PRESENTING THE SELF

Many teachers have said they became more certain about what they knew by teaching their knowledge. So, another method of "enlifenment" is communication. In the case of the Buddha, he began relating what he'd experienced to a few students. As he did this, he became clearer about what he knew. By teaching what he directly experienced, his knowingness became solidly integrated into his being. To explain this further, the more he spoke of what he experienced, the more he understood. The more he understood, the more qualities of his true nature he was able to experience. The more he experienced, the more he was able to be present in the fullness of his being and, as a result, he was able to teach more about his enlightenment. It was an expanding evolution of his consciousness: teaching, understanding, experiencing, and embodying. So, following his example, we need to spend time externalizing our direct experience through journaling, communicating, or teaching the experience to others in order to bring the awakening into greater presence.

COMMUNITY

The Buddha then created a *sangha*—a community of like-minded people searching for the truth—to align with fellow seekers. They didn't have to hide their aspiration for the truth. They supported each other through the barriers to enlightenment that the mind puts in the way and were accepted when authentic awakening occurred rather than being regarded as crazy. Students could seek the truth in solitary fashion—as it was traditionally practiced—but they did this together. *They had to do it by themselves, but they didn't have to do it alone.* Within this community, they could cultivate the skill of being in the true essence of themselves; i.e., practicing presence and bringing this beingness into the doingness of their lives (be you to fullness).

CLEARING THE MIND AND EMOTIONS

I'd like to suggest that had psychotherapy existed at the time, the Buddha would have recommended it for the following reasons. When enlightenment occurs, and even though the knowledge of truth remains, the high or the exalted state of perceiving our experience fades over time. For instance, if we've been to the Grand Canyon, we have the knowledge of what we saw and how we reveled in the experience. If we look back a few weeks later, the "high" is gone, but the memory is still there. Similarly, as time advances after a direct experience, the knowingness is there but the experiential connection is less. The personality isn't as strong as before, but it's still hanging around. It comes back in, and we can lose touch with the experience. However, we've had a powerful transformational event of de-identifying with the ego, and the neurotic fixation is no longer cohesive. As a result, elements of the ego begin to dislodge. This may take the form of surfacing memories, emotions, physical sensations, or trauma itself, as I described earlier. These can overwhelm us.

> *Enlightenment has then two sides: abiding in true nature and liberation from all rigid and fixed structures. In fact, the more one is liberated from ego structures and their patterning influence, the more one is able to abide in true nature.*
>
> — A.H Almaas, *The Inner Journey Home*

A major error on the spiritual path during these times is to use meditation techniques—such as concentration on the breath, a mantra, the guru, etc.—to force the meditator back into a calm state of equanimity to push away the emotional material that's been dislodged, hoping that "this, too, shall pass". In fact, what some meditators do is use their practice to separate themselves from or suppress what they're unwilling to experience. The calmness that appears to be there is actually the result of dissociating from the emotional body. It's the result of emotional dullness not emotional clarity. True equanimity is more the result of clearing the mind of its reactivity not enforcing emotional passivity, which comes from distancing ourselves from the emotions or sensations. When the mind is cleared through effective psychotherapy, the true self has fewer impediments to its radiance shining through.

The spiritual path isn't about being addicted to calmness or equanimity. It's about responding appropriately to the situation at hand without over- or under-reacting to resolve the presenting issue. If, for instance, I'm being attacked, I may need to respond to my attacker physically or run rather than be passively equanimous.

A good short-term block of psychotherapy sessions can be of tremendous help in releasing the hold of the ego and the reactive mind over the true self so we can present more of who we really are in our work, family, and all other relationships on the path of our true self-actualization.

> *"...meditation on its own is not particularly effective at solving people's emotional problems. It can prepare the ground, so to speak, by making the person more accepting and less defensive, but without a therapist's intervention, there is very real danger of paralysis."*
>
> — Mark Epstein, PhD, *Thoughts without a Thinker*

> *"...experience and recognition of true nature, regardless on what dimension of subtlety and completeness, do not automatically dissolve all ego structures. Unconscious elements of the psyche are not impacted by conscious experience directly, except maybe in exposing them to consciousness on some occasions. These structures are impacted only by awareness of them and complete understanding of their content. The Enlightenment experience may give the individual a greater detachment and*

presence that might make it easier for him to confront these structures and issues without being overwhelmed by them and have a better opportunity to work through them. The greater presence that may result might make it easier for the individual to abide more in true nature and in this way have greater detachment from the influence of the structures... But the structure will not self-destruct simply because the soul has seen the light."

— A.H Almaas, *The Inner Journey Home*

PRACTICING PRESENCE

Another important practice is the practice of self-remembering or "practicing the presence." This is a simple practice of placing our attention on our true selves, especially in our interactions with others.

The real difficulty in coming back into life after an enlightenment experience is that people will perceive us differently, judge us, and want us to conform to how they think we should act or how we used to be. They'll see a difference in us but, in reality, we aren't being somebody else. We're being more ourselves. We're presenting more of who we are and less of our social personality. So, we're paradoxically different but the same. This can be a major challenge after an enlightenment experience, as we can be tempted to abandon our connection to our true self in favour of contracting into our limited ego, fearing the judgments or rejection of others.

Being able to shift our point of view to let others have their critical opinions without taking them personally is crucial. As one of my retreat participants said, "If I'm a phony, it's inevitable that some people will like me and some people won't. If I'm real, it's inevitable that some people will like me, and some people won't. Since I can't get everybody to love me all the time, I'd rather be liked or disliked for being myself."

There's a saying: "There's a king or queen in all of us and, if we notice it, it will come out." So, the more we put our attention on ourselves—especially in the crucible of our relationships with others—the more we'll develop our ability to live from our divinity.

This activity of self-remembering takes courage, but it will help us bridge the gap between the spiritual and everyday life that many spiritual seekers feel is there. The ultimate test of the enlightenment experience is how we live it in life. When we courageously practice being present, we'll begin to see that life itself is our workshop and our spiritual path of self-mastery. There's no difference between the spiritual and ordinary life.

It's also important that we adopt and maintain an ethical lifestyle and vow to treat others well. All spiritual and religious traditions promote this component. If we do bad things to others—in our own estimation—we'll feel guilty and, out of this guilt, we'll hold ourselves back in life, including preventing ourselves from being more fully in life.

PHYSICAL HEALTH

Finally, it's important that we continue our personal growth through physical healing and spiritual practices. The body is said to be the temple of the soul, and if we aren't fit and healthy, we'll have difficulty presenting our authentic being. It's also important to continue our evolution through continuing to do retreats, workshops, and a daily meditation practice. Even though we've realized our self, there's still the project of directly experiencing what others are and what life, love, god, truth, mind, and consciousness are.

In summary, after a direct experience, the next phase is "enlifenment," which involves:

1. Being with your true self in meditation
2. Communication of your direct experience
3. A supportive community of friends

4. Psychotherapy, when required
5. Self-remembering in inter-relationships
6. Physical health and fitness
7. Continued spiritual growth practices

If this process of enlifenment isn't undertaken, and we remain satisfied with just having had the awakening experience without cultivating it in the ways I've mentioned, there's the real possibility that it can become lost. In addition, a phenomenon called "spiritual depression" can set in. It will be as if we've climbed to the mountaintop, reveled in the exhilaration of the glorious view of human potential, and experienced the deep fulfillment possible in life only to come down into the valley and see people with their noses to the grindstone. We see them bustling about, trying to survive in the never-ending necessities of life—people who are unaware of what it's like at the mountain peak—and living their "normal" lives. Our lives can no longer be "normal" because we now know the divinity in life, others, and ourselves. But because we haven't cultivated our awakening, there's too much of a discrepancy between the so-called spiritual life and real life. It's too wide of a gap to bridge, and hopelessness and depression could set in. So, these enlifenment practices are crucial.

> *"More often than not the ordinary mystical experience of expanded consciousness comes purely by chance, and since it is unconnected with a discipline for sustaining or enlarging it, it effects little or no transformation of personality or character, eventually fading into a happy memory."*
>
> — Philip Kapleau, *Three Pillars of Zen*

Chapter 8

TO GURU OR NOT TO GURU?

In our journey together, we've come a long way and discovered some new understandings and assumptions that help us determine if we need a guru and how we might progress best on the spiritual path. Let's look at what we've arrived at so far:

1. The purpose of the spiritual path is to become conscious of the truth of life, self, and others and to fully live from this basic reality.
2. Truth can only be experienced.
3. Overwhelming experiences (trauma) and socialization can block us from knowing the truth and living from our essential nature.
4. Awakening is the direct experience of the truth of life, self, and others.
5. After awakening begins the process of enlifenment.

Now, with this new understanding of the spiritual path and the nature of truth and awakening, we can finally tackle the guru question: Do we need a guru to lead us to our own direct experience of truth, free us from our overwhelming experiences, and assist us to live from the fullness of our essential nature? And, if we do, what kind of person would this be?

Let's begin by investigating what a guru is and go from there.

WHAT'S A GURU?

Traditionally, the word "guru" is used in the Hindu, Buddhist, and Sikh traditions to indicate a religious teacher. The word originates in Sanskrit and is formed by the syllables *gu* and *ru*. *Gu* indicates darkness and *ru* indicates destruction. Thus, when translated directly, guru means "dispeller of darkness." So, it appears that a guru is a spiritual teacher, someone who can dissolve the "en-dark-enment" or illusion in the mind of the student in order to bring them to the opposite state—enlightenment.

The question is: How do they do this? How do they dispel the darkness? How do they free us from our illusions? We need to get an informed answer to this question, since we run the risk of more delusion, or en-dark-enment, if we don't.

Does the guru wave a magic wand to clear the darkness, offer affirmations, hit us on the head, speak to us logically, convince us with scientific evidence that there's no darkness, or enlighten us with a special touch or gaze? Maybe they offer us their version of reality. We've already gone over many of the methods that don't bring us to the truth. These don't work, so how does a guru do this to us?

Let's consider a statement by a Buddhist monk in the Theravada forest tradition:

> *"The real basis of Buddhism is full knowledge of the truth of reality. If one knows this truth, then no teaching is necessary. If one doesn't know, even if he listens to the teaching, he doesn't really hear."*
>
> — Ajahn Chah, *Taste of Freedom*

Chah is suggesting that a student can't be taught how to know the truth unless they've already arrived at it. And, if they already know it, they don't need to be taught. These types of paradoxes are common on the path of enlightenment. What does this mean? How does a guru help a person get to the place where they know and don't need to be taught? There's an enigma here that's unlike anything else in life. In most realms of life, people can be presented knowledge and advice that will help them have better relationships, find more satisfying work, or be a more effective parent, but, in the spiritual realm, that intellectual understanding doesn't automatically transmit a divine experience of self. We're already clear that dogma or second-hand experience doesn't bring people to the first-hand experience of awakening. So how does a guru help us if not through dogma?

THE TRUE TEACHER

Once again, at the risk of creating more dogma, I'd like to suggest another assumption to explore—that the true guru doesn't do anything *to* us, but they do something *with* us. That something isn't dogma. It's a technique. The true guru is more like a coach, a mentor, or an advisor who teaches us a method and supports and inspires us to experience the divinity within ourselves, for ourselves. It isn't the guru's job to personally dispel the darkness within us. That's our job. If it were up to the guru, this would only create a dangerous co-dependency whereby we continually need the guru and, without the guru, we'd be lost. The guru can't dispel our darkness through intellectual discourse, affirmations, guided visualization, hypnosis, answers, etc. It must be done through something else. That something else is technique.

Now, at this point in our exploration, I'd like to propose that we change our label for this kind of person to indicate more accurately what we're speaking about. Words are especially important here because they orient us in the right direction. I'd like to suggest that we change the term that we use to describe this type of individual to another one—"spiritual guide"—and spend time exploring a definition that more accurately describes this person so, for once and for all, we have no more dogma gurus.

So, let's set out with this new definition, try one on for size, experiment with it, and, if necessary, change it later: *The spiritual guide is anyone that teaches us transformation techniques and supports us as we encounter the barriers on the path to enlightenment. The spiritual guide is one who supports us to release past trauma and illusions, to awaken to the way life is and the way self and others actually are, and to live from our true presence in life.* The true teacher leads us to the teacher within ourselves or our inner guru.

The Best Spiritual Guides – Techniques, not Dogma

In my opinion, the best spiritual guides are the ones that offer us effective techniques and a minimum (or none) of their own beliefs or dogma about ultimate reality. As we've already determined, second-hand belief systems limit us to predetermined spiritual experiences or get us caught in fabricating experiences that appear to be real but aren't. Far superior are spiritual techniques. These could be any method that facilitates our own insight and awakening such as journaling, art therapy, music, dance, contemplation, group interaction, communication exercises, etc. These are open-ended and devoid of anything designed to bring us to a predefined outcome. These modalities should be free of the teacher's belief system and proven through years of testing and modification to help the seeker open up to the truth for themselves.

Training

The spiritual guide shouldn't only offer techniques but also training in improving our ability and understanding of how to use these techniques. For example, we've heard the common, New-Age aphorisms, "*Follow your heart*" or "*Listen to your intuition.*" This sounds fine, but it's a recipe for seekers to get confused and lost. How can we follow our intuition if we don't have any training in how to do this? How many times have we heard someone report, "My intuition is telling me not to do this," when they're clearly just avoiding and resisting? God didn't tell them not to take advantage of an opportunity that could really help them; it was their fear of change. This is untrained intuition. I've seen far too many people back off from a wonderful opportunity for personal growth when it was presented because their "heart" told them that they should do this another time (and they never do). This is where many self-help books fail. They provide great ideas but not the experiential hands-on training. True spiritual guides not only offer effective techniques but lead seekers through step-by-step instruction that improves a person's ability to use the method. They also offer guidance and support to do the techniques optimally.

The best teachers coach you through the early and ongoing barriers as you progress through the various stages to enlightenment. (You'll read about these stages later in the book). They know the pitfalls intimately because they've personally fallen into them and progressed through them. They can teach you how to recognize them and not back away from them. Good spiritual guides can skillfully add their ability to yours to inspire you to face some of these crises and get through them in a balanced way and in a fraction of the time it would take you to do the technique on your own. In addition, the spiritual guide's presence is often an inspiration in itself. The strength of their presence gives us the confidence that we, too, can awaken in spite of the significant obstacles.

Natural

Although this can sometimes be hard to evaluate, techniques should be natural. They should be based on the way human beings and life naturally unfold and evolve in consciousness. The best techniques emphasize or focus on these natural dynamics to accelerate the process that organically occurs in life. So, instead of taking lifetimes for a person to make a breakthrough, it can occur in a matter of a few months, days, or hours. A good technique should allow a balance between seekers following their own unique path to the truth in their own time and being encouraged by a facilitator to evolve at a quicker pace. If there's too much forcing by the seeker or the facilitator, it could create resistance or a retraumatization of the individual and set the person back in their evolution. Too much forcing can, in some cases, cause purification energy in the body to be released before the person is ready.

Earlier, I mentioned a technique for banishing unwanted thoughts that involves the person thinking a negative thought and banging their head against a wall 144 times to remove it. This is unnatural—not to mention painful and potentially dangerous. There are breathing techniques that can concentrate too much life energy (or pranayama) in a person's body and cause psychosis. This, too, is unnatural.

On the other hand, a common Buddhist practice of mindfulness meditation is based on gently putting one's attention on the breath to quiet the mind. It's part of the mind's organic tendency to investigate and inquire. So, use of this technique is very effective.

Optimal methods involve a balance between the gradual dissolution of emotional traumatic material and erroneous mental concepts and, at the same time, opening us up to the opportunity for divine insight to occur. As this psychological material is cleared, there's less in the way of us recognizing our true nature. When we directly perceive our true selves, there's new space in our psyche for our essential being to fill. The mind then has less illusion to sort through to digest and can better integrate the awakening into a new understanding. If our cup of erroneous beliefs is already full, we have no space available for truth to occupy. Without letting go, there's less opportunity for letting in realization and letting out the radiance of the true self.

> *"All the prophets, seers, sages and saviours on the world's history became what they became and consequently had the powers they had through an entirely natural process. They all recognized and came into conscious realization of the oneness with the Infinite Life."*
>
> — Ralph Waldo Trine, *In Tune with the Infinite* (1897)

I once encountered an individual who told me that his guru's main method of awakening was to notice when he was having a negative thought, immediately set it aside, and think of a positive thought to replace it. The student of this guru appeared to be very apprehensive and almost paranoid about his mind and was constantly on the lookout for thoughts he labeled as negative. At the same time, he seemed to have a glow about him, but the glow seemed almost manufactured. I warned this individual of the danger of this technique, suggesting that he was merely labeling and judging certain thoughts as bad and wrong and suppressing them. He disagreed and continued with this practice daily. Years later, I met a friend of this student who told me he'd been admitted to a mental institution with symptoms of a deep psychosis that displayed itself as demonic possession. This seeker had, in essence, relegated all the so-called negative aspects of himself into a rejected part of his psyche. Over a period of time, this compartmentalized aspect of himself became a persona that he condemned as evil. Eventually, the pressure that was built up inside this sub-personality surfaced and created an immense amount of suffering for him. The practice he'd been taught was unnatural because it artificially labeled certain natural emotions as unwanted and others as desired.

In addition, the best techniques shouldn't create dependency on some outside mechanism or substance to open us up to direct experience. It's okay, for instance, to start off using a guided meditation from a teacher or a CD, as long as the program is training us to eventually practice the technique on our own. The same goes for certain hallucinogenic plant medicines and chemicals such as LSD, marijuana, and ayahuasca. Individuals can often have divine experiences on these substances, but, because people haven't arrived at these experiences by themselves, they can develop a dependency on or even an addiction to them if they're overused. When used occasionally—under professional guidance in the context of psychotherapy—in a clinical setting—the insights and divine experiences that result can be life-changing. The Canadian physician, Gabor Mate, has done some amazing research using ayahuasca to liberate people from alcohol and drug addiction (https://drgabormate.com). However, if these substances are used too frequently and without discretion, they can bypass an individual's normal healthy defenses and coping mechanisms and release reactive and traumatic material in the mind that they may not be ready to deal with, causing an imbalance in the psyche. Overuse of these substances overrides our ability to choose to be open or closed down. Some people end up stuck in being open to negative forces and are unable to close them off.

Part of any good natural awakening technique involves a process of clearing away the reactive mind in a grounded and balanced manner so awakening can spontaneously occur in its own time. When it does, integration of the awakening experience can happen in a more balanced way as the new sense of self is incorporated into those areas of the mind that are clear. Dissolution of the reactive mind prepares the ground for the seed of awakening to be planted and to grow. External mechanisms employed that are outside the seeker's control can leapfrog over the neurosis of the mind into the land of enlightenment without the necessary mind-clearing work that needs to be done. This clearing work creates new, open space in one's being for new spiritual awareness to shine through. Without this work, the seeker can feel separated from their direct experience and get stuck in a spiritual depression caused by having an exalted illumination but being unable to live from it.

It may be hard to judge whether a technique is natural. I'd like to suggest that if a technique is drawn from a process already in life, the practice of it will automatically bring us more into life. In addition, since life is primarily lived with others, it will bring us closer to others. Over time, some techniques create a schism in which the spiritual life appears as separate from normal life, or seekers begin to feel they're alienated from others. These symptoms indicate a problematic technique. A natural technique will open us up to the growth potential in just living our lives. A natural technique draws us into life in such a way that we're more willing and able to face its challenges and the everyday contact with others.

Structure

True guides not only offer techniques and training in how to optimally use them without the hindrance of dogma, but they also provide structure to support the efficacy of the technique. Structure could consist of a conducive environment, a schedule, agreements that create emotional safety, disciplined practice, or an ongoing support group. It's exceedingly difficult for individuals to open up and face the deeper aspects of their humanity and the human mind in a chaotic environment. Details like a distraction-free, well-ordered retreat setting, a scheduled routine to keep people on track, agreements of confidentiality and non-evaluation of others provide a container that enhances a sense of safety, focus, and security. Protected by this container, we can then throw ourselves into the disciplined application of what's being taught without having to continually handle the usual distracting influences of life. Structure could also relate to a daily or weekly routine of practice, follow-up programs, and ongoing events that keep an individual progressing incrementally. This steady progress can help stabilize and embody awakening experiences and allow opportunities for further breakthroughs to occur.

Contact

One of the most overlooked aspects of any technique is the teacher or, more accurately, the awakened presence of the teacher. Something immeasurable and magical can happen when there's a deep rapport and connection between the student and the spiritual guide. If the guide has awakened and had several profound enlightenment experiences, the guide will be relating to us from their true self with an awareness of what we actually are. The guide can connect from their true self to our true self. Even though we may not be conscious of our true essence, the teacher is, and she can connect with us on that level. As she sees us in our divine nature, that contact stimulates our awareness of ourselves to grow. We might say that these kinds of spiritual guides are catalysts of consciousness.

There is a principle of consciousness at play here: whatever a person consistently puts their attention on in life, they get more of. If we see the good in our children, the more likely it is that they'll be good. If we see the bad, the more likely it is that they'll display that. The same is true with a spiritual guide. As the spiritual guide is aware of us in our divine nature, so, too, we become aware of ourselves. This experience often occurs in silence and without anything being done. Yet, without anything being done, something *is* done—the activation of a deeper awareness of ourselves.

This contact, when combined with the compassionate presence of the guide, creates trust within the seeker and, out of that trust, we begin to feel the safety to allow ourselves to reconnect to our true nature—that essence we had to hide or suppress in childhood when we learned that it wasn't okay to be ourselves. In this space where we're being embraced within the gaze of unconditional love, we allow ourselves to grow. This phenomenon is often called *darshan* in Hindu culture and, in Western psychotherapy, it's often referred to as the "therapeutic use of self." It's this divine contact that can accelerate the process of any technique.

> *"The lesson for psychotherapy is that the therapist may well have as great an impact through her presence as she does through her problem-solving skills... this kind of silence is what allows us to repossess those qualities from which we are estranged."*
>
> — Mark Epstein, *Thoughts without a Thinker*

QUALITIES OF AN AUTHENTIC SPIRITUAL GUIDE

U-n-I-versal Guides

Whether or not you choose to be supported by a spiritual guide, the following are some essential qualities that I suggest this individual should embody. This list has been developed over years of being with spiritual guides, through observation of the many spiritual teachers during my time at the Ecology Retreat Centre in Ontario, and through a survey of people on my mailing list.

1. **Awakened and non-dogmatic.** Has this person successfully been to where you want to go in your spiritual development? Have they themselves awakened? Do they demonstrate a wisdom that indicates they know the human condition and the nature of existence, or is it just book learning? "Successful" doesn't necessarily mean they're a millionaire, as that kind of "success" is in another realm of life, but do they at least have a balanced life including having awakened? One of the keys to getting to where you want to go in your self-evolution is to work with someone who's been where you want to go. It means they've achieved what you want to achieve, and they know how to get there. Has the guide had deep awakening experiences beyond dogma or only awakened within the particular belief limitations of their lineage teachings? Enlightenment is often a process of unfolding awakenings over time into deeper depths of union with the ultimate, where we open up to divine paradoxes that get resolved as we penetrate the depths of the opposites. We may experience the non-existence of the individual self and then later directly perceive that there's a universal self beyond the idea of non-existence itself. We may open up to the emptiness of clear consciousness only to find that on a deeper level there exists the fullness of divine love within it. We may suddenly see that the material universe outside us is an illusion and doesn't exist and then later experience that it doesn't exist outside ourselves because it's all within us. The best spiritual guide uses techniques that are open-ended and have no specific goal other than to awaken us to whatever direct experience is there—not to a direct experience that confirms a religious belief system. As I mentioned earlier, many genuine

enlightenment experiences can be denied because they don't fit the dogma of the teacher or because the teacher didn't have these experiences themselves. It's best to be with spiritual guides who've penetrated these paradoxes. The value is that they're open to any awakenings that may occur in us and are able to recognize them. Their recognition can help draw these experiences out so we won't lose them.

2. **Experienced and trained.** What kind of training and experience have they had? Have they had extensive training and a lot of experience in the method they're using, or have they just taken some weekend course and decided to give a workshop? Have they gone through an apprenticeship or tutorship that included a lot of supervision, or are they self-appointed experts? How many retreats over how many years have they given? What are the participants of their retreats like? Are they the kind of person you'd like to be? Are they balanced, kind, compassionate, less reactive, etc.? How many of their students have awakened (as defined by the standards I've described of direct experience in this book), and how long has it taken them to awaken? If the guru has thousands of students and very few have awakened, why would you want to study with them? We should be impressed by the results a guru gets, not the long lineage he represents. In any other of realm of life, we'd be a good consumer and look at the quality and quantity of someone's service. We should do the same in the spiritual marketplace!

3. **Empowering Human Mastery.** Do they see the spiritual path as part of everyday human life, or do they see the human realm as something that needs to be endured and somehow transcended? Do they encourage you finding wisdom in your own life, or do they focus on attaining some kind of esoteric state removed from normal life? The best spiritual guides see no difference between the spiritual life and ordinary life. They see us all as

part of the collective fulfillment of existence. They encourage mastery of the mind, relationships, health, and finances, even though they may not teach all these subjects. They lead you to see the divinity here and now rather than somewhere else in some later time. They see the reward in living and being more engaged in the here and now rather than finding fulfillment in some other realm. Do they lead people to find the wisdom and self-understanding within themselves or offer quick-fix answers that keep students dependent on the guru? Are they promoting themselves as a saviour or encouraging others to save themselves? A true spiritual teacher will encourage you to be responsible for your own life—even to the point of making you face your own victimhood rather than create a false sense of pity that only keeps you stuck. They inspire and motivate you to find the resources within yourself and your own life rather than create a dependency on them. Do they welcome questions and being challenged on their assumptions and ask their students to make their own decisions?

"A guru can only point the way; he/she/it is NOT the Way. A sign on a highway shows you the direction to your destination; it is not the destination."

— Ron Dankowich, astrologer, Orangeville, ON

4. **Morality.** Does the guru have a moral code of conduct in how they treat their students? If there are agreements or rules of conduct that they ask their students or retreat participants to observe, do they follow these or consider themselves to be exempt? How do they behave around the opposite sex? Do they relate naturally or invite inappropriate flirting or sexual innuendos? Do they promote any ethical or moral standards to live by?

5. **Coherency.** Are they coherent? Do they demonstrate in their behaviour, relationships, and work the kind of life that you'd want to emulate? Do they walk the talk or just give good advice while the rest of their life is in shambles? Do they follow the guidelines and practices they preach to others?

6. **Humanness.** Are they human? Have they been banged up on the spiritual path and overcome their difficulties? Have they developed wisdom from their experiences? Often the best guides are the wounded healers—the alcoholics who've recovered; those who've gone through physical, sexual, and emotional abuse and have healed; those who've experienced the deep despair of life and found the light at the end of the tunnel. Do they know what it's like to lose a loved one or have a relationship break up or to become seriously ill and recover? Do they demonstrate human uniqueness and individuality? If they've experienced a lot of suffering, have they healed? Have they done their psychological work? Psychological health indicates that the techniques they've used on themselves are effective. Can they share some of their own mistakes and errors in life and use these as teaching experiences, or do they present an aura of perfection? This humanness is an important quality because these kinds of guides have empathy and patience with you on your path. What are their beliefs about emotions? Do they believe in a healthy expression of emotions in a way that trauma can be released and healed, or is there a fear of emotions? Do they deny or denigrate the emotional world? If so, they may lead us down a dangerous path of suppressing or dissociating from our emotions.

"A good teacher/guru/trainer can be an invaluable resource. They are, however, human beings, and it's most useful to see them as such. If I put someone on a pedestal and then

they show themselves to have human frailties, it is I who has pushed them off the pedestal, since I put them there in the first place."

— Jonathan Kramer, Dynamind instructor,
Newmarket, Ontario

7. **Compassionate.** Are they compassionate or critical and judgemental? Are they coming from a place of sincerely wanting to help others out of love and concern, or are they self-interested? Unconditional love is important for us so we can feel safe to enter into the tender areas of hurt and let go of suffering. Compassionate direction from a spiritual guide invites our uniqueness and authenticity to gradually surface through the neurosis of the ego rather than encouraging us to condemn our imperfections with the hope that this will eliminate these characteristics and cause the true individual to emerge. Do they judge you for making mistakes or help you let go of your self-recrimination and guide you to find the lesson in your error?

8. **Humility.** Is there a lack of ego in the teacher or a manufactured charisma? Is there direction to exalt and accept yourself, or is there a sense of them promoting their own adulation? Even in their humbleness, is there a sense of natural radiance, happiness, and peace of mind that naturally comes from within, or is it somehow pumped up? Are they uniquely themselves or presenting the commonly accepted persona of the "guru" in their speech and actions? Are they accountable? If they make a mistake, are they willing to admit it, apologize, and learn from it, or do they hide their errors or, even worse, blame others or the group for their lack of spiritual advancement?

9. **Sense of Humour.** Do they have a sense of humour, or is there a stoic rigidity about their demeanor? A sense of humour is

a sure sign of being connected to one's true self. Those that are enlightened take themselves lightly (because they have less baggage to weigh them down). They can see the ridiculousness of the erroneous attachments and ego misidentifications that trap us and, in so doing, can help us laugh at it all in a way that brings a sense of spaciousness and a new understanding of our human condition. They exemplify the deeper joy and happiness of being free from the mind and being connected to the aliveness and contentment that inherently resides in the true self.

"When I think of dogma, I think of rules or beliefs. Sometimes it is subtle and sometimes not so subtle. Several years ago, I believed I had found the path for me and my long, drawn-out search was over. I loved the meditation technique I had learned, and I experienced such huge shifts in my life that I decided to become a meditation teacher myself. Part of this experience included taking vows to my teacher at the time. I was taught (and it is scary teo say, that I also believed it) that having him as a teacher was the one and only way to Enlightenment. In my vows, I surrendered my life to him. He was very charismatic, charming and manipulative. Luckily, after a few years, I left that teacher and that path. I am grateful for this experience. I learned many things—including what I want and what I do not want.

"Alarms go off for me when I see these similar traits in a teacher or a teaching. I am not interested in anyone telling me how to live my life; what to wear; what to think or who I can have a relationship with. If a teacher wants control, that is the first sign that there is something wrong. In my opinion, a good teacher is one that encourages you to discover the true teacher within. They do not want control, and are not focused

on getting money, power, fame, or sex. Also, I'm not looking for a teacher who is full of charisma and can perform on Broadway. I'm looking for someone who is there to serve humanity very humbly... someone who comes from a place of authenticity, and who has a solid experience of the truth.

"There are many 'wolves in sheep's clothing' out there, and most of them have similar characteristics that I have mentioned. It is so obvious to me when I see them now."

— Diane Yeo, meditation teacher,
London, Ontario

Chapter 9

THE CONSCIOUS SEEKER

We've come a long way in our investigation, and I want to thank you for persisting with me in this journey together. We've looked at what the spiritual path is, what truth is, what blocks us from awakening, how we can and can't experience the divine, and what the true spiritual guide is and is not.

But there's one glaring thing missing in all of this investigation: US!

What's our responsibility in all of this? I'd like to suggest to you that this is where the focus of most of our investigation should be. If we've had bad experiences with gurus, are we victims? How can we be accountable so that we have good experiences?

I believe the solution for navigating our way through the spiritual marketplace is to learn how to become a conscious seeker. This isn't something we can become right away. It's something we need to learn. This type of learning is very much like leaning. Just as we lean on a bicycle until it moves or lean on the side of a sailboat to straighten it up, so, too, we can lean in the direction of an ability that we want to learn. If we force too much, we may become too fanatical in the other direction. The term "leaning" implies being gentle with ourselves as we make an effort. We don't want to make so much effort that we put all our attention on the action and miss what we become aware of as we engage in the new learning experience.

LEAN TOWARD RESPONSIBILITY

This may sound like some fluffy, New-Age truism, but the fact is, we're all 100% responsible for what happens to us in life. This doesn't discount that there are people in life who try to hurt or take advantage of others, nor is this a way of using spiritual bypassing to avoid opening our hearts in an uncompassionate way to others by saying, "You're responsible," or, "It's your karma." Look at leaning in the direction of, "I'm responsible for what happens to me on the spiritual path," as a way of eventually freeing ourselves from suffering. Even if we can't take responsibility for the trauma that's been inflicted on us by others or by a guru, we can at the least try to be accountable for the limiting conclusions we've made up about life, others, and ourselves as a result of these events. Even though bad things happen to us in life, we're still the ones who decide how to hold or view these incidents. No one reaches inside our heads and turns the choice-making switch on. We're the ones who choose.

I know about this all too well.

My Journey to Self-Responsibility

For many years, I suffered from the infidelity of women, feeling trapped in work that I hated, being scammed financially by others, and being a part of two cults where there were sexual, financial, and power-dynamic abuses. I felt like I could never get ahead in life. Early on in my spiritual path, the shadow side of my personality started to rear its ugly head. Memories surfaced of six weeks of physical abuse and abandonment when I was in the hospital as a two-year-old, of physical trauma by a neighborhood boy who abducted me when I was three, of several incidents of sexual abuse when I was seven, and of numerous disappointments involving my alcoholic father. I couldn't believe that I caused all of these situations. "How could I, as a young, boy cause this?" It was inconceivable that an innocent young boy made this all happen. I got angry at people's glib responses to my story: "Oh, you created this!"

But I leaned on this idea: "I'm not a victim; I'm responsible".

The first thing I asked was one of the most important questions I've ever asked myself: "As a result of these incidents, what belief did I make up?" I was aware that I'd made up certain beliefs: "I'm no good," "I'm unlovable," "I'm alone in life," "I can't get what I want," "My needs aren't important," "I'm a victim," and others. Even though I was young, I realized that no one forced me to make these things up. It was the inner consciousness within me that needed to make sense of the abuse and try to explain it all. I did this innocently because I didn't know any better.

So, I worked through therapy, meditation, and the co-evolution process (described in a later chapter) and was able to dissolve these beliefs. It was these beliefs that caused later experiences in my life. Even though I couldn't see how I attracted the abuse, I saw that I created the future experiences of betrayal and victimization through my beliefs. But I kept leaning on the thought, "I'm responsible," and, over the years, images and memories of past lives surfaced. I recalled one past life as a Nazi officer, which explained that the abuse in this life happened because, in that past life, I inflicted pain on others. I needed to experience the effects of abuse so I'd become more conscious of and compassionate toward others. I saw that the man who had an affair with the woman I loved, who tried to secretly destroy my business, and who almost drove me to suicide, was a man whom I'd deceived and killed in a past life. We'd been getting even with one another for many lifetimes—but getting even only made us odd.

I was able to forgive these people and myself and let go of these recurring patterns. In the process, I continued my spiritual search and had enlightenment experiences that gave me the deep knowingness that, throughout all the abuse that had happened to me, the essential me had always been untouched. Nothing could destroy who I was. My true nature was still pristine, pure, and unsullied. In a very practical way, these deep awakenings allowed me to heal. So, the understandings that have liberated me didn't come from some superficial new-age theory. They came from blood and guts on the path as well as relentless investigation.

As with everything else I'm presenting, I suggest that you lean on the idea that we're responsible for everything that happens to us on the spiritual path. We need to be accountable for the decisions and actions we take or avoid taking. We need to be wary on the spiritual path and not blindly trust someone because they have a white beard and a saffron robe. We don't know what's "arising" underneath that robe or behind the backdrop. We need to remember that if someone is in a body, they have stuff to work out. They aren't perfect yet. Trust needs to be earned.

LEAN TOWARD BEING YOUR OWN GURU

Lean on the idea that the ultimate spiritual guide is inside—that is, you. Even though you might be exploring the path of Buddhism or Christianity, you aren't inherently Buddhist or Christian. You're always you. We're always the true self. Our identity isn't the religion. We're just putting on the personality of the "ism" or "ity." To put on a label is to get trapped in that label. Ultimately, each one of us is the truth itself. How could we recognize something is true unless it was already in us? There must be an inner reference point from which to compare it. Each one of us is that reference point because each one of us is the truth. Hold the idea that the only reason something occurs as being true is because it is the inner guru (Gee You Are You) that's verifying it. It's the existent truth within us that's comparing what's said by the teacher on the outside with the teacher within. Don't accept this because I say it. Lean on it, and, one day, when you're graced by divine experience, it will appear as a reality and free you.

Lean on the idea that the true spiritual path is your life. There's so much wisdom in our lives already; it's so obvious that we miss it. If we can take this point of view, even if we're on a specific spiritual path, we can open up to the greater inspiration that may not be part of the tradition we're trying out for a while. Restricting our unfoldment to only the tradition we're exploring can lead to the viewpoint that "there's no spiritual growth in everyday life." In fact, life is the testing ground. If we want to find out how centered we are in equanimity, there's no greater test than facing someone yelling at us when we innocently cut them off in traffic or being with our young daughter who's having a temper tantrum in a public place. There's great learning in life. Lean on the idea that there's nowhere else to go. This is It! *Life is our spiritual path.* And since our life is the ultimate spiritual path, we should continually be looking for the wisdom we've found in it. "What did I become aware of today?" "How did I grow in greater ability to be and present my true self today?" are wonderful questions with which to end the day.

Even though we're ultimately our own guru on the spiritual path of our lives, we should, paradoxically, be a good student. This means acquiring as much understanding of the philosophy and as much training in the techniques presented as possible. We should be passionate about our learning, asking questions and not going on to more learning unless we've fully understood what's come before. Maybe you'll be drawn to become a spiritual teacher yourself. The best teachers have always been the best students.

> *"Like the bee, gathering honey from different flowers, the wise man accepts the essence of different scriptures and sees only the good in all religions."*
>
> — *Srimad Nhagavatum* – Hindu spiritual text

LEAN TOWARD YOUR DOGMA DETECTOR

We should learn to recognize when dogma is present so we can decide whether we want to accept it or not. Here are some recommendations:

The first thing we need is to get clear about, is what dogma actually is. Right from the beginning, we shouldn't accept anyone else's definition of dogma—even the one I offer. I'll offer my own definition, but it's best if we each develop our own. From this deeper insight, we'll have an understanding of the features of dogma from which to recognize it. If it's perceived, we can consciously decide to reject, accept, or suspend it. (A way to develop your own definition is to do the co-evolution exercises on dogma in the back of this book.) For the sake of exploration right now, I'll offer my own definition of dogma: **a set of fixed, second-hand beliefs that we (or the person communicating them) haven't experienced as being true.**

There's an intractableness about dogma that indicates: "This is the way it is, and there's no other way." There's no alternative view. There's no room for debate or discussion. There's an illusory certainty about it as the person delivers it. As a friend of mine once said, "She's got it all together. She's like concrete… all mixed up and permanently set." One may well ask, "Isn't there certainty when one directly experiences the nature of one's true self? What's the difference, then?" Yes, there's certainty, but this comes from union with the truth. It comes directly from one's self. There's an inner authority. With dogma, the surety is propped up by an external standard. The person who uses dogma is hiding his/her own uncertainty in the vicarious certainty of their teacher or their "sacred" scripture, almost like the wimp talking tough while hiding behind his giant friend.

To detect dogma, the question to ask is: "Is there evidence of rigidity here that's reinforced by an external authority?" As you do this, you'll be able to identify when dogma is present and then to accept it, reject it, or put it on the shelf for further consideration. Here are some specific examples of rigidity:

- **Rigidity of belief:** Notice what the person, system, or religion uses to validate their beliefs. As stated above if, they use an external authority (their great saint says it's true) or they appeal to the number of years of their tradition (it's been around for 1,000 years) or they refer to the rule of the written word (the sacred scripture says it's true), we can assume it's dogma. Often people will say a belief is true because they have faith in it and no amount of argument or presentation of an alternative view can dislodge them. The argument is circular: "My faith has made it true, and I believe my faith is true." Often people will say they've experienced a belief system to be true when in fact they only "experienced" an intellectual understanding of it. It makes sense to them. It's the same "party-line" reproduction of reality that's propounded by their scripture, therapeutic system, or teacher. There's a "hole-lessness" to the holy party-line via which any variation or lack of coherence to the philosophy can be explained. There's no aspect of existence that can't fit into the religious container in spite of the fact that it's leaking all over the place. There's nothing that's unknown and, therefore, the wonderful mystery of you and me together in the universe is dry and dead. All wonder is gone. Any opposition to the dogma is met with over reactive righteous indignation or the admonition that non-believers are less advanced spiritually. It's all part of the socialization structure that ensures conformity and is a sure indication of dogma.

"True Religion is sensitivity to reality."

— J. Krishnamurti

- **Rigidity of language:** Are there terms that are used over and over in spiritual discourse (e.g., non-self, ego, karma, non-duality, holy ghost, sin) to explain spiritual phenomena but little originality in the use of this terminology? Certain concepts ebb and flow in and out of "New-Age" and religious culture. They come into vogue like fashion statements, and people present them out of a manufactured spiritual personality, but the foundation of it all is jargon. Remember that words are powerful, and certain terminology used over and over can, solidify a religious "party-line" doctrine. As we know, names are labels and can limit our experiences to certain belief prescriptions and exclude others. Notice if there are common words used over and over. If so, this indicates dogma. However, if there's other terminology employed that creatively expands these concepts or introduces subtler spiritual understandings or a unique iteration, we can conclude that there's a genuine spiritual experience being communicated. Even so, taking on the unique terminology of others—even if it originates from that individual's own direct perception—just creates dogma within us. We should take the time to develop our own personal insights and direct experiences, and be wary of limiting our own concepts of self and consciousness to jargon.

- **Rigidity of attire:** Strict adherence to a particular dress code often indicates adherence to a set of beliefs. This is certainly obvious with established religions where a dress code indicates a respect and an honouring of the tradition but, at the same time, fosters conformity to that tradition. Certain styles of clothing or common dress (e.g., white shirt and tie) can also serve to socialize followers into a dogma. There may be different attire for the leader that denotes a certain level of spiritual attainment that may not have anything to do with their level of consciousness.

When I owned a retreat center, I recall serving a group who set up our meeting hall as a holy temple. I was asked to put a hat on my head before I went into the hall as a gesture of respect for their guru and tradition. A month later, a different spiritual group came to the center and set up their meditation hall. I was asked by the monk to take off my hat before I entered the space. I imagined the potential discord if these two groups ever shared the same meeting hall, each arguing over whose hat or lack of hat was more sacred, missing the whole point that it isn't the sacred objects that make *us* holy, it's us imbuing the object with our own reverence that makes *it* holy. This act of respect is essentially a reminder to create in our hearts the necessary attitude to establish a sacred container for the worship and spiritual practice that occurs in that space.

- **Rigidity of emotion:** Those stuck in a dogma may have a limited or even low emotional response. Emotional dullness is often equated with calmness. Spontaneity or a fuller expression of emotions may be held back with the belief that emotional expression, even laughter, is wrong. Excessive seriousness can be evidence of dogma. Those who adhere to a dogma can be more in their minds than their hearts and can use their beliefs to avoid a compassionate response. They can even use the dogma as an excuse to mistreat others. Spiritual bypassing or using spiritual concepts as a way of dismissing the suffering of others or avoiding taking responsibility is common with dogma. Phrases such as, "Well, that's her karma," "If it's God's will, it will happen," "He created this himself" are common. People stuck in dogma tend to default to these empty aphorisms when they lack the courage to venture into the unknown world of just being with another in their suffering and experiencing that intimate moment when we truly touch another on a soul level.
- **Rigidity of hierarchical structure:** Is there a hierarchy of passing down a belief system, (e.g., Pope to bishop to priest) or a generational hierarchy from one generation to the next? There will always be some variety of indoctrination into a system of dogma in a hierarchy. Wherever there's a structured bureaucracy, belief has to be encapsulated in order for it to be transferred from one generation to the next, and dispute is less tolerated. Often the reason there are schisms in religion is because someone in the system has had a deep insight or divine experience that doesn't fit the prescribed belief construct, and they have to leave to avoid persecution.

"The dogmas of the quiet past are inadequate to the stormy present."

— Abraham Lincoln

I'd like to suggest that, even if many ancient hierarchical traditions carry dogma within their teachings, we shouldn't automatically dismiss them. This would be like mowing down a flower garden because it has a few weeds in it. Part of the reason that a tradition may have existed for so long is that there's an actual basis of ultimate truth and a genuine foundation of effective techniques for awakening. There's great value in studying these traditions and their age-old literature and being guided by a teacher for a period of time. Before one has had awakening experiences, one can use these teachings to point the way—as long as one is able to identify the dogma. Another value in studying these traditions is being able to recognize in these teachings descriptions of enlightenment experiences similar to our own after we've awakened. This can help to discount any doubt in the mind about our own enlightenment experiences and validate the awakenings.

Just because a tradition is dogmatic doesn't necessarily mean we should reject the teachings (just as we shouldn't accept them). The teachings may, in fact, be an accurate description of reality; we just don't know they're true because we haven't had our own direct experience of them.

This task of "dogma-detecting" is a necessary skill on the path of the "Conscious Seeker." It's no easy task, and it's not for the faint-hearted. It requires the courage of a rebel and a renegade—not in the sense of facing an outward tyrant but in facing our inner victim, the one who so easily accepts the theoretical hearsay of others rather than be with our own reality.

> *"We must approach life as though stepping from a dark chamber into a lighted one for the first time, without anticipation or expectation as to what we are to see or hear and then subject each experience to our own analysis, not coloured with the analysis of others. The person who really*

wishes to approach the mystical life in a frank manner... must not be a coward. He must not hesitate to oppose or challenge tradition."

— Ralph M. Lewis, from the book *The Sanctuary of Self,* AMORC (Ancient Mystical Order of Rosea Crucis)

LEAN TOWARD THE UNKNOWN

This is one of the hardest things to do on the path of transformation: being willing to hang out in not knowing. In our culture, there's a lot of investment in being certain. We need to do business with people that know their profession and understand what they're doing. We want to work with people that can give us predictable results. We've been educated to be an expert in a certain field and to be proficient and clear about what we know and what we do. Our employ-ability depends on it. Knowledge is power. Knowledge is money.

But, in the realm of awakening, knowledge is actually an impediment. It's a barrier. If we're to find the truth, we must go beyond our present knowledge. We must go beyond the boundaries of what we know, because we don't know what we don't know. We also don't know what we need to know. And, to know the truth, we must give up what we now know so we have a fresh openness for any new deeper insights. We must give up the barrier of the old to find the new. When we hang onto our old knowledge, when we set out into the unknown, the mind manipulates the new knowledge to fit in with the old. It will overlay the old understanding on the new experience and interpret the present experience with the eyes of the past.

To find the truth for ourselves, we don't have to say we're wrong or stupid or deluded about what we know; we just have to set our concepts of reality aside for the time that we're investigating. Instead of being afraid of the unknown, we replace the fear with openness and curiosity, as if we're seeing through the eyes of a child.

We should approach our search for truth with a sense of wonder and fascination: "Wow, this is a new experience—one that's similar to another experience but totally unique and new. What's this all about?" We're like a scientist observing an experiment with intense interest. To do this requires an extraordinary sensitivity to take in all the nuances in our inner and outer perceptive field. It requires a new skill of receptivity and of moving with and adapting to every shade and colour of reality. And, as we do this, we'll find the heaviness of old knowledge falls away, and we move into a new lightness of being. A new deeper sense of satisfaction arises in us as we enter into a new world of wonder with a heightened sense of openness and curiosity. It's as if we've found a new life, a new evanescent vitality in which there's a deep satisfaction that comes inherently out of the natural desire to inquire into our true nature. In reality, this activity of mindfully observing and taking in experience is what all beings in life are doing anyway: being alive and wanting to know all there is to know of this existence.

> *"Your time is limited, so don't waste it living someone else's life. Don't be trapped by dogma-which is living with the results of other people's thinking. Don't let the noise of other's opinions drown out your own inner voice… and most important, have the courage to follow your heart and intuition. They somehow already know what you truly want to become. Everything else is secondary."*
>
> — Steve Jobs

As we develop this skill of being with things as they are, we see the tyranny of dogma—how dogma makes us dull and contained and replaces our aliveness with something deflated and dead. We see how those who settle for dogma settle for a reasonable facsimile of life to avoid the fear of the unknown—even though, on the other side of the veil of the unknown, there's a world of experience, full of the delight of continual newness. Once we've tasted this new spiritual manna, we can never settle for dogma food again. There's no comparison. Just living life in this new openness becomes inherently fulfilling. Existence becomes its own reward.

We should cultivate being okay in the zone of the unknown. We let ourselves know that we don't know and are okay with this. This doesn't mean we're dolts; it means we're explorers. We should try to detect any belief or point of view about reality that we haven't experienced as being valid and ask, "How do I know this to be true?" "Do I know that past lives exist? Angels? Karma? Akashic records? Chakras?" "Is there a non-self or an Atman (supreme self)?" "Is there a God?" We shouldn't accept anything until we've had the experience ourselves. One of us could be the only person in history that proves all other sages wrong or maybe directly experiences an aspect of reality or a different view of truth that no one has ever seen before (and start a new movement). After all, this is what the Buddha did.

We should avoid rejecting or accepting any belief but rather take it on as an assumption that it may or may not be true. Let it be tentative. We could look at it as a possibility—like everything in this book—being skeptical but not to the extent of being cynical and rejecting. We need to hold up every point of view about reality that comes our way for later inspection. But if we take in beliefs without examination, there's little chance of the growth of a new insight and self-awareness, little growth of real intelligence. It's the lazy way. It's the way of cheating in the school of life by writing down somebody else's answers in the mind.

When we suspend the dogma, we increase our potential for more insight to occur in our lives. We have more material for our future experience to connect to and to integrate. The more material we have to connect to, the more we integrate our new insights and the more solid our new awareness is—as in the phenomenon of bissociation we explored earlier in the personal insight section.

Many of us have had epiphanies in which we've exclaimed, "Ah, yes! Now I understand. That explains it all. This now explains that, explains this, and explains that. I thought I knew it all, but now I really understand it!" It's an event in which a new insight or even a direct experience connects to other suspended thoughts and feelings that powerfully come together. So, dogma is valuable insofar as we neither accept nor reject it but rather hold it out until our own insight allows us to understand it with new awareness.

Secondly, when we communicate our new awareness, we should try to develop our own language for our experiences as much as possible. We can default into the terminology of many ancient traditions, but there's a great value to developing our own language. We explored in a previous chapter the importance of our presentation and the struggle of accessing the right words to communicate our inner realms (even though the wording is still a description, not the real phenomenon) as a way of drawing out that experience and integrating it. This helps us embody or live from our self-realization. Ultimately, our unique explication is the very gift the world needs to expand our collective evolution. It's a factor in the co-evolution concept that we'll explore in a later chapter.

> *"Mind speaking truth through the lips or thinking truth consciously can bring all the satisfaction to the world which the world is seeking. Nothing material can strengthen people, but the omnipresent can strengthen them with all the power of truth."*
>
> — Emma Curtis Hopkins, *Scientific Christian Mental Practice*

Our biggest challenge on the spiritual path is to continually monitor whether we're taking beliefs, points of view, ideas, or concepts as the truth when we haven't experienced them ourselves. We need to vigilantly discriminate clearly between knowledge or understanding and "knowingness"—namely, that which we actually know through our own experience. This practice will be rewarded, eventually, with profound insights and inspirations that spontaneously come out of "know" where. Once we have a taste of this divine experience, there's no going back. We'll see dogma for what it really is—a ghost hiding in the shadows trying to convince us it's the light, when we now know the sun shines within us. Our own brightness is our gift to the world.

> *"The truth of Illumination is found through honouring every person's right to have personal truths, following the voice of his or her own Spiritual essence... ignoring the rigid human rules that evolve when one human wants others to follow the leader instead of the voice inside."*
>
> — Jamie Sams, *Thirteen Original Clan Mothers*

Finally, there's one more thing we need to consider to be a conscious seeker, and it's probably one of the most important.

LEAN TOWARD PERSONAL PSYCHOLOGICAL WORK

Many years ago, when I was the owner of the Ecology Retreat Centre business near Orangeville, Ontario, I was asked to deliver a bowl of fruit to the cabin of one of the spiritual teachers who was running a two-week meditation retreat. He was a Buddhist monk from the Theravada forest tradition.

I was going through a bit of a spiritual anarchist phase at the time and, when I knocked on his cabin door, and he opened it, I said irreverently, "Here's your fruit, sir. Do I have to bow down to you before I give it to you?" He laughed, and we were instant friends! I'd recognized one of his challenges as a guru. He asked me to come in, and we had the most wonderful conversation about the conflict he was having in honouring his tradition by wearing robes. He confided that the robes engendered an idealized fantasy in students' minds of a perfect, realized teacher that he had to frequently dispel by reminding them he was human, too! (I think he even passed gas when I was talking to him.)

My Human Meeting with an Exalted Man

About 30 years before this encounter, I had a beautiful human experience with the Dalai Lama before he became famous. He'd just escaped from Tibet, and he came to Canada for his first tour. He gave a talk in the Tibetan language in a small meeting hall in downtown Toronto. His interpreter did a poor job, and we hardly understood a word he said. After the talk, the Dalai Lama's entourage was clearing a small path in the crowd so he could exit. During the commotion, I was somehow pushed right in front of him. I didn't know what to do, and, in shy embarrassment, I automatically put out my hand and said, "Hello." There was hush in the audience as if some sacrilege was about to happen. A mortal was going to touch this ideal holy man. Suddenly, the Dalai Lama stretched out his hand to me, shook my hand, bowed to me, and laughed uproariously. Everyone in the crowd laughed along for about two minutes. It was the most wonderful lesson to everyone: to treat the most holy man as if he's human and to treat the most human person as if he were holy! In spite of the fact that no one understood his talk, that small gesture to me has been the most enduring message of this man's life.

Yet, so many spiritual teachers and students get caught in the trap of idolatry. Why? Teachers may create that image and juice us with their charisma, but, *we go along with it*. If we put a guru on a pedestal, they topple off, and we get hurt, who's to blame? Remember: I suggested that we're all 100% responsible.

There are two further issues I'd like to suggest you consider. The first is the reality that many spiritual teachers have awakened to the state of unified existence to varying degrees, and we feel the radiance of their clarity, serenity, joy, and love. We're drawn to them because the connection to their true essence is causing us to get in touch with our own essence. We're unconsciously resonating to the vibration of their conscious connection to themselves. We're attracted to what they're aware of in themselves because it's in us, but we aren't yet noticing that it is. They're reflecting back to us what we are. We can get enthralled by this and, if we aren't careful, we can only see their divine presence and ignore the fact that they're human beings with frailties, neurotic tendencies, and human desires. We may believe they're flawless, and maybe we forget to notice that they burp, go to the bathroom, and think about sex like the rest of us. We may ignore our intuition that something about the way they act isn't quite right. We may believe their dogma is the truth and deny our own experience. It's these human factors that can hurt us just like any other human can hurt us. Yes, we should honour and respect the wisdom they present to us, but we must also honour and respect ourselves because, on the level of ultimate truth, there's no higher or lower. There's no hierarchy. There's only the one truth that's the same for everyone to experience whether it's you, the Buddha, Jesus, or me.

The second issue is getting caught in the trap of idolizing a teacher because we haven't done our inner psychological work. Maybe we see in the teacher the ideal parent we never had. We may desperately want to experience the unconditional love we missed as a child so we can grow into the person we might have been, but, if we haven't done our personal work to let go of our early trauma, we'll still be unconsciously acting as children. We may attract a guru whom we let violate our boundaries in unscrupulous and abusive ways just to get that love. We repeat the same victimization that we experienced in our childhood with our parent(s). When the guru falls off the pedestal and onto us, it's a nasty way to begin personal work. The student can be re-traumatized to the extent that they're hurt for the rest of their life, and they may never, ever recover.

We should also realize that being in a relationship with a teacher by accepting his/her beliefs—without investigating their veracity—is essentially an immature relationship. It lets both the teacher, and us, off the hook. We don't have to do the work to find out the truth on our own, and the teacher doesn't have to do the work to lead us to our own self-realization. In a way its a dual addiction. We get addicted to having a guru and the guru gets addicted to having followers. It takes effort and candid discrimination to be liberated. Freedom isn't free. It requires persistence, patience, and focused effort.

It also takes discipline and compassion on the part of a true spiritual guide to let go of teaching dogma and support the seeker in awakening. They must deal with individuals in a journey of purification. They enter into the world of the reactivity of the human mind. The true teacher often holds up a mirror to the seeker, who'll resist seeing the shadows in themselves and, instead, project their neurotic patterns onto the spiritual guide. They're tested to stay connected to their true presence in the face of this abnormality. The real teacher knows that the craziness of the human mind is very compelling yet sees the divinity in all of us. Out of compassion for our suffering, the real teacher jumps into the cesspool, but, as guides, they must also do their own personal work.

Most people on the spiritual path are attracted to the light of the fire on the path, but they don't want to face the heat. The deep psychological work of trauma and core-belief clearing is essential for us to become whole. This work will help us reclaim what we've neurotically tried to find in the guru: the rejected parts of ourselves and our self-love. It will open the space for more expansive awakening and self-integration to occur and help us avoid attracting these types of dogma gurus. We need to walk the journey of awakening as an adult, not as a co-dependent child.

"It takes courage to grow up and be who you really are."

— E.E. Cummings

In summary, here are suggestions for becoming a Conscious Seeker:

1. Be 100% responsible for what happens on the spiritual path.
2. Be your own guru, and take on life as your spiritual path.
3. Be really clear about your personal definition of dogma (second-hand knowledge) and learn to recognize it.
4. Be willing to ask this important question with any new spiritual concepts to which you're exposed—"Do I really know this to be

true in my own experience?"— suspend what you don't know to be true, and hang out in the unknown.

5. Do your psychological work.

As we approach the end of this chapter, I hope you understand that I'm not recommending that you don't have a teacher. That's your decision. I've found some teachers profoundly valuable and, conversely, found others to be damaging. You may find, as I have, that teachers are important at some point on the path for a short while—or a long while—and then, at some point, they're not. But let's discriminate between dogma gurus and spiritual guides, and let's be responsible for how we interact with them. Let's be wary of how we create a relationship with them out of our own unmet childhood needs. The same rule in the consumer marketplace applies in the spiritual marketplace: Buyer beware.

In summary, we've investigated many of the illusions and traps on the spiritual path and come to some new understandings. I hope, as I've mentioned several times, that you (with the assistance of the exercises at the end of this book) arrive at your own insights. I'm not interested in becoming another dogma dispenser. I'm more interested in exposing the assumptions and beliefs that keep us trapped so we can look at these clearly and avoid them. With this in mind, I'd like to expose one more assumption—one that's consistently held us hostage in a big way—and use this as a segue into the next chapter.

IS THERE AN ALTERNATIVE TO THE DOGMA GURU?

Over the centuries of spiritual seeking, there has been a relatively unexamined curious assumption: there's no alternative to the guru/student relationship. It's always appeared to be the only way to truth. Trying to go it alone has been too hard. Many of us, as serious seekers, have assumed that the only way we can get to the door of awakening on the spiritual journey is to follow a guru, and part of the trade-off is to put up with the dogma. We take for granted that dogma is part of the guru package. Perhaps even the guru has forgotten this.

We've felt there's been no choice. Just like someone who's desperately thirsty will drink polluted water just to quench his thirst—even while knowing the water may hurt him—so, too, have we ignored teachings that are tainted with dogma just so we can get the instruction and guidance of the teacher. But is this true? Do we need to get into bed with the guru and go all the way or part of the way or none of the way? Is there another option?

I'm here to tell you that, yes, we may need spiritual guides to teach us techniques to one degree or another, but there is and always has been an alternative. It's always been with us, and it can lessen our dependence on a guru and allow us to be more self-reliant.

The existence of this alternative is so obvious it's shocking. When you see it, you'll slap your forehead like Homer Simpson and say, "Duh!" When I saw it for the first time, I did the same. I almost put a bruise on my forehead. I was excited about this discovery because, just like you, I'd put up with dogma for years and years, thinking there was no other way. Now, I'm passionate about the alternative. It's why I'm writing this book—to reveal it to you. In my estimation, it's one of the most overlooked aspects on the spiritual journey. And when you realise it, it will give you inspiration, excitement, and greater freedom to choose to have a guru or to find the teacher in yourself or, at any time, to choose both. This alternative is called co-evolution. It hangs out in the place you'd least expect it to be: YOUR LIFE.

Chapter 10

CO-EVOLUTION

Co-evolution means things **evolving** together in relationship with one another. Co-evolution isn't something new; in fact, it's the fundamental basis of reality. It's a natural principle of life that's occurring whether we're aware of it or not. Once we become aware of it, we see it's obvious in an infinite variety of manifestations.

Darwin was one of the first to notice this dynamic, although he described it in terms of physical evolution. He observed that plants and animals adapt and change according to the influences exerted on them by something in the environment outside themselves. The change that occured was always with respect to being in relationship to something else. For example, the chameleon developed the ability to camouflage itself as the result of predation by other animals. The bat developed its method of sonar detection to locate the insect prey that came out at night to mate and feed. Flowers developed interdependency with bees whereby they provided food (nectar) for the bees and the bees in return spread their pollen. This interrelationship, through which all things adapt, develop, and grow, is everywhere in life. Nothing develops in isolation and, the reverse is also true. Anything that remains in isolation won't evolve and will eventually die. So, in a physical universe, co-evolution exists.

But does co-evolution exist on a metaphysical level? Can it be the basis of reality? Is it connected somehow to the growth of consciousness? What is it in our existence that causes us to want to know the truth of ourselves to facilitate self-realization? We're now going to take a close look at this phenomenon. It's called life.

Let's explore this with a simple exercise of the imagination.

ALONE IN THE U – N – I - VERSE

Take away everything outside of you in the universe. Take away the planet. Take away the sun and the stars. Take away other people. Take away even your body. If there were just a non-physical you and nothing else, how would that be? If you were born that way, prior to the existence of anything, into a world with nothing to interact with and nothing to experience, what would be missing?

I'd like to suggest there would be no knowledge of anything in your mind—because there would be nothing to experience—there would probably be no thought, because there would be no experience to think about. (As we examined in an earlier chapter, knowledge and thought are the result of experience and, because there would be no experience for the mind to organize, knowledge wouldn't exist.) You'd only have pure consciousness, empty of content. There would only be you, empty awareness, and no method of experiencing yourself.

How would that feel? Imagine. It would probably be very lonely... maybe even intensely lonely. You'd probably have no sense that you even existed. You might even wonder if you were in a dream or a figment of someone else's imagination. You'd probably want to know if you existed or not, right? Maybe there would be an urge to find out who you are or to know yourself...to gain some self-knowledge.

If so, what would you want to do in that state?

You'd probably want to interact with something outside yourself, to give you some sense of yourself, to have a real experience.

Now, add in the physical universe, including your body, but without people. Imagine you're now interacting with the sky, trees, the soil, and the entire natural world. Because you'd now be engaged in experiencing, knowledge would start to form. You'd learn about the foods you could or couldn't eat, animals that were safe or dangerous, the best way to survive, etc. You'd develop knowledge about ways to improve your life. You'd have to adapt to that world by interacting with it. You'd learn about the world by the mistakes you make and the successes you have. Your adaptation would be the result of your knowledge of the world and resultant conclusions about ways of being and actions you could or couldn't take. You'd be developing not only knowledge about the physical world but some self-knowledge. You'd start to understand what you're capable of and the potential you have.

But would the loneliness still be there? It probably would. You'd still be all by yourself and wondering if you exist… wondering who you are. You'd probably come to the conclusion: "The only way I'll know that I exist is if something outside of myself, similar to me and just as real as me, could interact with me and verify my existence. It wouldn't work for me to just interact with trees or chickens or apes because, if I did, I might conclude I'm a tree, a chicken, or an ape. I need something remarkably similar to me." That would be a great revelation. You'd want other humans in your life.

So, go ahead and add other people into the world. Now the real drama begins.

Interactions would go up maybe 1,000-fold along with your experiencing. Imagine how much you'd learn about yourself that you didn't know before. Knowing little about others, you might innocently mistreat them. Conversely, you might have very pleasant experiences. They might love you. You'd learn that you can be hurt and what it is that hurts you—e.g., abandonment, lying, abuse, neglect, judgement, cheating, manipulation, etc. You'd learn you want to be loved and to love others. You'd learn you want to be treated respectfully and to treat others well. You'd experience what it's like to be understood or not understood. You'd have to look inside for the self-knowledge of how you want to be treated and learn how to communicate to make others aware of what you want. You'd have to acquire a clearer knowledge of yourself to relate this.

You'd develop an affinity with others that share similar self-knowledge. You'd form relationships. In the deep caring and bond that others would have for you, you'd learn that you exist. You'd want others to treat you in a way that demonstrates you're as real as they are… not as an object but as someone with an internal human world similar to theirs, with the same cares and concerns. You'd experience wonderful joys and intense suffering. You'd innocently take on the mistaken ideas that parents, friends, or your culture have about you because you want to be accepted and loved. You'd probably lose a sense of yourself, form an ego, and someday learn that self-love and self-acceptance are more important than others' opinions of you. In this loss of self, you'd ask, "Who am I, really?" and begin to search for a way to become more conscious of who you are, what life is, and what others truly are to find an understandable context for all your suffering so you could lessen it and maximize the sharing of love.

I could go on with this exercise, but it illustrates the huge difference between existing in a world alone versus in a world full of relating to others. The difference is the amount of self-knowledge and awareness that's developed. It's important to note that this self-knowledge isn't growing just in you and no one else. It's growing collectively. As we interact with others, we cause them to grow in awareness just as they cause us to grow. We evolve together. This is a co-evolutionary process! We do it by ourselves, but we don't do it alone!

MY PERSONAL AWAKENING TO CO-EVOLUTION

Let me expand on this concept of co-evolution by sharing a direct experience that I was blessed to have many years ago. It occurred in a meditation session as a student in the Rosicrucian Order. Years later, it was deepened at a retreat called the Enlightenment Intensive.

I was, on both occasions, intensely contemplating the question, "What is life?" and trying to directly perceive its essential nature, when, all of a sudden, I lost the sense of myself as an independent self.

I became conscious of myself as the being of all beings… the universal being behind all of existence, everywhere, in all things physical, non-physical, and in everything manifested—even in that which dwelt in pure potential. It was expansive and exhilarating, and I felt as if the purest light was pouring through me and radiating out of my body. I was, paradoxically, God and myself at the same moment. I was that universal essence but, at the same time, I was my individual self. I was non-dual and, at the same time, singular. There was no one else in the universe but me. I was it. I was God, and God was me.

I was there just before creation. I was alone, wondering if there was anyone else out in the universe. I was aware of a fundamental capability of my true nature—I had free choice. In fact, I was choice itself. In that state of aloneness, I noticed that I had the ability to know everything but, in fact, knew nothing about myself even though the capacity of infinite self-knowledge was there. I was innocently un-self-aware—and the very first instance of self-awareness was: I became aware that I wasn't self-aware.

Out of my free choice, I chose to ask the question, "Who am I?" and I realized that, to answer that question, I needed something outside of myself to see myself. I needed something to act as a mirror. At that instant, I split myself into an infinite number of other individuals, each of which was the same God that I was. They were the same universal god as me with the same infinite potential, but each one had an individual point of view. They were like me, in that each one of them was me yet they didn't have the same awareness of their individual selves and each other. They were fully conscious but had no knowledge of themselves, just as newborn babies are fully conscious but have no experiential knowledge of their new world. We all had the capacity to view and reflect back to one another our differentiated perspective, but the singularity of each of us as individuals was vitally important. We needed to be slightly different from one another to accentuate and mirror each other's each unique aspect of our god self. If we were all the same, we couldn't notice all these aspects and become more conscious.

In this differentiated state, we could see each other in ways we couldn't see ourselves. In our difference, we could, over eons of time, come to know the totality of our universality. And, in order to evolve the knowledge of our god nature, we needed one important dynamic: to interact in such a way that we could bring each other to greater consciousness. So, we began to relate to one another. It took eons, but, eventually, through experimentation, we developed a method of doing this: something called communication.

We were one being divided into many unique individuals, relating to one another and creating as many ways as possible to communicate for the sole (soul) purpose of becoming conscious of our true nature. We were doing this all together: co-evolving.

This enlightenment experience isn't unique to me. It's echoed throughout much of ancient and modern spiritual literature. The following are some writings on this subject.

> *"The Sufis often quote the hadith, or extra-Qur'anic revelation, in which God says, 'I was a hidden treasure; I loved to be known, so I created all.' God wants to know (His) nature, (His) possibilities, (His) manifestations. This love to know (Him) self, the desire to know (Him)self, appears in us as the love to inquire... One way of understanding the situation is that God's love of revealing the divine manifestation appears in us as love for the Truth. These two loves are the same thing; for ultimately there is only one, undivided reality... This clarifies what the ultimate service is. You do not work on yourself to become Enlightened; you work on yourself so that God can do what God wants to do, which is to reveal (Him)self. So our delight in investigating reality is an adventure of consciousness, which is the human participation in God's enjoyment of self-revelation."*
>
> — Almaas

"We are the means by which the universe is getting to know itself."

— Thomas Berry

"Far away in the heavenly abode of the great god Indra, there is a wonderful net which has been hung by some cunning artificer in such a manner that it stretches out infinitely in all directions. In accordance with the extravagant tastes of deities, the artificer has hung a single glittering jewel in each 'eye' of the net, and since the net itself is infinite in dimension, the jewels are infinite in number. There hang the jewels, glittering like stars in the first magnitude, a wonderful sight to behold. If we now arbitrarily select one of these jewels for inspection and look closely at it, we will discover that in its polished surface there are reflected all the other jewels in the net, infinite in number. Not only that, but each of the jewels reflected in this one jewel is also reflecting all the other jewels, so that there is an infinite reflecting process occurring.""

— Francis Harold Cook, *Hua-Yen Buddhism: The Jewel Net of Indra*

"In the beginning, that which Is, is all there was and there was nothing else. Yet All That Is could not know itself - because All That Is all there was, and there was nothing else. ...Yet the experience of itself is that for which it longed... so All that is divided itself—becoming in one glorious moment, that which is 'this' and that which is 'that'... Now in creating that which is 'here' and that which is 'there,' God made it possible for God to know Itself. In the moment of this great explosion from within, God created relativity—the greatest

> *gift God ever gave to Itself. Thus, relationship is the greatest gift God ever gave to you."*
>
> — Neal Donald Walsh, Conversations with God

> *"All forms of life and being are simply variations on a single theme: we are all in fact one being doing the same thing in as many different ways as possible."*
>
> — Alan Watts, Does it Matter?

AWAKENING WITHIN SUFFERING

For months after this initial awakening, I had additional insights into our co-evolutionary universe (these corollary epiphanies often accompany an enlightenment experience). I became aware that if we were all individual gods and each expressing the infinite potentialities of the universal God, we obviously had the potential for infinite power. I questioned what would happen if these divine individuals began relating to one another without the awareness that they had such power. I looked to the planet for an example.

It was clear what would happen, because it was already happening. There was all manner of relating—from despicable and evil depravity to beautiful and elevated sacredness. There was all manner of personalities—from Hitlers, Idi Amins, and Stalins to Gandhis, Martin Luther Kings, and Mother Teresas. There was extreme victimization of the poor, raping of the environment, and slaughter of the helpless. Yet there was great philanthropy, sacred arts, music, and uplifting spiritual practices. It became clear that in our unawareness of each other as divine beings with infinite power, we'd manipulated and overpowered one another. We didn't fully know what we were doing and how we affected each other. In our innocence, we inflicted terrible suffering and trauma. We experienced the demolition derby of bashing into one another in the victim/perpetrator game, trapped in the terrible confusion of it all.

But at some point, we began to wake up. Down through the ages, in our countless interactions, we communicated the effects of our manipulation and injury to each other. As our communications were completed, we learned to understand. We emerged from our trauma and healing began. We stared across in horror at the person we'd just killed in war. Maybe we returned in another life, and they killed us. We learned that others aren't objects; they're just as real inside as we are to ourselves. We took the risk to really contact one another on a deeper level and discover the divine love that we all intensely feel for each other.

Incrementally, we learn that we're all interconnected and entwined in this inevitable relationship called life, where the only activity that matters is the communication of ourselves. And, with every action of relating, the most amazing thing is happening—we're evolving in self-awareness, love, and ability. At some point, we get that it's all sacred, emerging from the mosh-pit of life and moving into a divine square dance as we finally realize we're all gods playing a hide-and-seek game—with you hiding in me, and me hiding in you.

"Forgive them, for they know not what they do."

— Jesus Christ

So, co-evolution is a condition of life. It's part of the nature of existence whether we know it or not. It doesn't depend on us knowing it's happening for it to happen. Co-evolution is occurring if we have a guru or if we don't. It's happening if we're on a spiritual path or not. It's happening even if we try to avoid life by running away and living in the woods. We'll still be in relationship, even if it's an avoidance relationship. We're evolving along with everything else in the universe in an interconnected web.

Once we view life through this lens of co-evolution, it becomes clear: Doesn't our greatest personal growth occur in close relationships? Of course! We're drawn to be in groups, friendships, and intimate relationships because it's in the relating that happens in these collectives and pairings that the inherent purpose of life—which is to expand our consciousness—is fulfilled. That is where it expands the most. Just like all streams naturally flow and join to form rivers, and rivers naturally flow and join for form lakes and oceans, so do we naturally want to converge and communicate ourselves in relationships. The flow of our true nature is to become more conscious of others and ourselves. This isn't a passive activity. It's an active process. We're doing it full-on whether we're aware of co-evolving or not. We can't escape it. Just as a fish can't live out of water, we can't exist without others.

When we let the *aha* of this insight settle in, it radically changes our lives. How? Not by altering it or changing it but by all of us accepting it. This acceptance transforms our life by bringing us into harmony with the nature of life. Every bit of life is spiritual unfoldment. There's no difference between ordinary life and the spiritual path. This difference is just a mental construct. Every time we complete a communication to another and receive someone else's communication, we aren't only singularly contributing to the uplifting of ourselves and that other, but we're incrementally contributing to the co-evolution of the vast web of creation. To see this is to realize the vast importance of each one of us in the U-n-I-verse and our contribution to the massive unfoldment on the planet. Life is where it's all happening. This is IT. It's *all* sacred… the whole shebang— you, me, them, and everything. We are saviours of each other! We are our own gurus!

So, if co-evolution is what's going on in life, is there a way of enhancing this process so we evolve and reach enlightenment much faster? Is there a way we can heal the suffering that our lack of awareness of each other has caused? The answer to both is yes. To fully answer this, we have to understand more specifically how co-evolution operates, and then we can apply this knowledge to accelerating the process.

"Mother, I have sought truth and I have learned that all living things create new traditions when they honour the sacredness found in the individual as well as in the whole of creation. I have experienced the clarity of their knowing when they desire understanding as much as they desire the breath of life"

— Jamie Sams, *Thirteen Original Clan Mothers*

Chapter 11

COMMUNICATION AND CO-EVOLUTION

Let's first explore how self-knowledge and understanding develop within the co-evolutionary universe so we can see how this natural process can be enhanced.

Without going too deeply into the philosophy of cognition or how we come to know anything, I'd like to suggest some ideas (at the risk of presenting more dogma). Once again, these ideas are subject to your own investigation. (I advise you at some point to do the Thought Clearing exercise on "Knowledge" in the back section of this book to come up with your own ideas.)

From my observation of life, I've seen that co-evolution occurs in a cycle that starts with a conscious decision to relate and moves through contact, speaking, listening, and then mutual understanding. After the cycle is complete, it may begin again. Let's investigate this cycle together.

The Decision to Relate

There are many individuals on the planet—billions of them. We pass them on the streets, at work, in restaurants, in parks, etc. They're everywhere, but we don't relate to all of them. We overlook the majority of people in our lives. Within the context of co-evolution, however, we're all here for one reason: we want to relate to others in order to become more conscious. This is a given. It's the nature of life. It's the way it is. If someone is in life, they inherently want to relate to others even though they may be unconscious of this fact. We're lucky that there are so many others available to relate to, but it's hard to engage with all of them.

We start with a thought in our mind that we'd like to get across to another person. There's something about us that we'd like another to become conscious of. Because that thought hasn't been delivered to another person, it remains suspended in our mind. (We've all had this experience of something we really wanted to say to another person and, because it wasn't said, it kept circulating around and around in our mind.) We start by choosing someone (or a group of others) to relate to. Even though we aren't conscious of the purpose of being in life with all others, we consciously choose a particular someone with which to engage. I look over at Betty and think, "I'm going to talk to her." Betty can choose to relate to me because she has a choice, too. If she doesn't want to relate to me, communication can't occur. Some people miss this fact. Sometimes, they force or manipulate others to relate to them when the other doesn't want to.

Fred wants to be by himself to figure out what's going on with him, and Jenny keeps telling him what she thinks is going on. He doesn't want to talk, but she keeps trying to get him to talk. Eventually, he gets so angry at her persistence that he tells her off and walks out. Trying to force communication can lead to any number of problems: abuse, resentment, acting out, anger, sadness, etc. So, it's important to understand that people mutually choose to relate to each other. This is where co-evolution all starts.

Contact

The next thing that happens is, we decide to connect with the person. We contact them. I go over to Betty, who recently started working in my office, put my attention on her, and try to engage her: "Hello, there," I say. If she, in turn, chooses to interact with me, she puts her attention on me. We put our attention on one another relative to our current awareness of each other. If I think Betty is just a body, I put my attention on her as a body. If I think Betty is more than just a body—that she's a conscious individual—I put my attention on her as this. If I think she's divine in nature, I put my attention on her as that. Anyone who's interacted with a holy person can sense the qualitative difference between someone seeing you as just a body and someone seeing you as divine. So, we establish some level of rapport based on our present awareness of what others are.

Within this contact, there are two components: the choice to trust and to be open. The trust is two-fold: trust of others and trust of oneself. Betty may have had some interactions with men that weren't so good, so she may be suspicious of me, being a man, and not trust me completely. Then again, there may be something in my authenticity that she feels safe with and, as a result, chooses to take the risk to trust a bit more than she normally does. She may also have a high level of ability to communicate with men and, therefore, trust that if the communication gets weird, she can manage to extract herself from it. So, she may not trust me, but she's confident of her ability to make the interaction safe for herself. Her trust is higher than someone who has a lower level of ability to interact with men.

According to the degree that we feel safe with others and our own ability to create safety, we choose to be fully open, less open, or closed. I may decide to be fully open to Betty, but she may be suspicious of me if I'm a stranger and decide to be less open than I am. Depending on our openness with one another, we decide how much of ourselves we want to share or how authentic and real we want to be. The reality of ourselves is often the most delicate, tenuous, and sensitive part of our being. Once again, this is all dependent on choice. Each one of us decides to connect with others to the degree that we choose to trust and be open to one another. The choice to contact another to be open and trust can't be forced upon us by others. When we honour another's choice to relate to us or not, and they recognize this, we automatically start off with more openness and trust.

It's important to note that there's a field of two opposites in which we must make choices: Will we be rejected by others, or will we be overwhelmed by them? These are the two fundamental fears of life. If we aren't accepted by others, we'll end up being alone. On the other hand, if others overpower us, we'll close down and contract within ourselves. We'll withdraw from others and also end up being alone. (This is the trauma experience that we explored in Chapter 4, Barriers to Awakening.) In both cases, we end up back in the original state of being in "solitary confinement" in the universe and unable to become conscious. We don't want to be solitary in the universe because we need others in our long journey of awakening to become conscious. Being alone is contrary to this purpose. This is where the whole "big bang" started, and we don't want to go back to square one.

Speaking

Once contact with another is established, we translate our internal experience into words and try to get them across to others. Let's say I've had an experience of being outside in the cold when it was hailing. To successfully communicate this, I first go through a process of constructing my message. I start by placing my attention on the full experience, noting all its components. I make distinctions between all the elements. There's being outside and being struck by hail, wind, wetness, body sensations of coldness, and shivering, and then there's the colour and size of the hail, etc. I go through a process of associating all of these with prior experiences in my memory, searching for individual words and concepts connected to these, and, from those, I compose my message. This inner contemplation may take only a second, or it may take a longer period of silence. Once it's done, I communicate in words using the appropriate body language and vocal inflections to get across my experience to Betty: "It's god-awful cold out there. The wind is blowing hailstones around the size of mothballs. I'm wet and shivering!" Even though words are merely a representation of my experience, I try to get across my experience with words.

Listening

The listener, being open, then receives the thoughts that were communicated. This involves an inner process, as well, of sorting and constructing. Betty hears my message and distinguishes all the separate words and concepts in my communication. There's a sorting process of drawing up from memory her experiences of coldness, wind, shivering, wetness, etc. She puts these together into a composite image that matches what I communicated. When she does this, she may actually have a similar experience as I had. When there's a match between my representation and Betty's, we can say that mutual understanding or consciousness has occurred. What I communicated and what she received are the same.

Acknowledgement

The communication cycle, however, doesn't end here. There needs to be recognition on the speaker's part that the listener understood the communication. In some way, the receiver needs to indicate to the speaker that they understood what was communicated. We may indicate this with a nod, a smile, by saying, "I got it" or "I understand," by repeating back what was said, or a number of other ways. Betty may say, "Wow, you really got hit by bad weather; let me get you a blanket to get warm." When I see that Betty received exactly what I communicated about myself, there's mutual understanding. She received exactly the thoughts I sent, and I recognize that she received them.

When mutual understanding occurs, a magical thing happens—the thought I started off with that was hanging in my mind disappears. It's no longer occupying my attention. It's gone, and there's now more space in my consciousness. The minor tension behind the desire to be understood by another has been relieved. I may feel closer to Betty and perhaps some deeper communication can happen as a result.

We've recognized a new experience, made new connections in the mind, and expanded our awareness of one another incrementally. There's a sense of fulfillment in this basic act of becoming a little bit more conscious of one another, because that's what life is about. We feel an inherent sense of satisfaction when we learn anything new or acquire a new skill. In a similar way, when we understand another person, there's that same feeling that we're fulfilling the purpose of life in our interaction.

Now what would have happened if I didn't get my communication across to Betty? What if Betty just ignored me? My thoughts would have stayed suspended in my mind and, because it's our natural tendency to want to relate to others, I'd have to use some of my internal energy to hold that communication back. My thoughts would be pushed into the area of my mind where all the other uncommunicated thoughts are crowded and, like a computer that slows down when thousands of e-mails are stored in the inbox, my effectiveness as a person would be compromised.

This is the fundamental reason why we suffer in life. To one degree or another, we've been traumatized, criticized, ignored, forced, or hurt by others who aren't fully conscious of who we really are. We haven't been given the safety and opportunity to have another person understand our experience of these overwhelming events, and the only thing we can do is hold back our thoughts and emotions with any number of coping mechanisms: denial, suppression, fogging, minimalization, shame, etc. We must do something to hold these communications back: take on a "nice" personality and be the way Mother wants us to be, make up a fictional explanation of "I'm unlovable" to explain Father's harsh criticism, or be sad like depressed Grandma, hoping that if I'm like her, she'll like me. It takes a lot of energy to bury these communications, but they don't die. They get buried, and they stay alive. There's a reactive charge to them and, when we meet people and experiences similar to those from the past, this charge gets released, and it creates further havoc in our relationships.

Yet, the potential to complete our communications is eternally there because, as we explored, if anyone is in life, they're here to relate and evolve in relationships. We're compelled, unavoidably, from the very essence of our divine nature, to get closer to one another.

Deep down inside, we're yearning to heal our past, be understood, and find people and circumstances with which we can do this. When we find these special people, we can choose to risk again, be open, get our withheld communications across, be received, and achieve mutual understanding.

If enough mutual understanding occurs with a few people, affinity and love develop. We can start to feel safe to share the more vulnerable aspects of ourselves. More satisfying engagement happens, allowing us to not only process and let go of our withheld pain but take the risk to investigate and communicate to each other the profound mystery of our true nature.

Under special circumstances—such as an extended retreat where communication among individuals is structured so people are being understood and consistently completing deeper levels of authentic relating—we can extricate ourselves from our socialized personality and heal our deepest traumas. As the ego masks fall away, and we're seen as we really are, the real possibility of recognizing our true nature becomes available. Direct experience can occur and, when it does, the mind is massively transformed. The fiction from which we've been living is annihilated. Truth is realized and becomes the basis upon which we can start living a new life.

THE COMMUNICATION CYCLE

In conclusion, it appears that co-evolution moves through a fundamental process that starts with a decision to relate, to another individual and contact is made. This progresses through a cycle of:

1. Sending thoughts (or communicating) after a brief period of contemplation.

2. Receiving thoughts or listening.
3. Acknowledgement or mutual understanding.

"Knowing together produces a new level of surprise...a brand-new Awareness."

— Richard Chester, PhD

What this means is that each individual act of being understood or understanding others is a spiritual act. Receiving and giving the authentic message of ourselves to one another is a small sacrament in the service of our own evolution—an act that we overlook in our deep desire to live an exalted spiritual existence. This ordinary act of everyday life could be evolving us far more than the solitary spiritual practices we've assumed are the only way to awakening.

So, if relating to one another is fundamental to the development of consciousness, the next question is this: is it possible to speed-up this process of co-evolution so that we can evolve in self-awareness more rapidly than in normal life? Is it possible to use this process so we can come to our own insights and awakening without the influence of a dogmatic guru? The exciting answer is, "Yes!" and that's the subject of the next chapter.

Chapter 12

CO-EVOLUTION AND THE DYAD TECHNIQUE

We ended the last chapter with a question about whether or not we can speed up the process of co-evolution so we can grow in self-consciousness much faster than ordinarily happens in life. Can we take this natural dynamic and duplicate or arrange it in some way that it's still doing its thing of evolution but more rapidly? Yes, we can, and, to do this, we have to improve two aspects: the quantity and quality of relating. We need to do this by enhancing the way co-evolution occurs (as discussed in the previous chapter)—through a communication cycle.

THE QUANTITY AND QUALITY OF RELATING

It goes without saying that the more communications that are completed between individuals, the greater the mutual understanding and therefore the greater the self-awareness. This is fairly obvious—more complete relating equals more personal insight.

The second aspect, the quality of relating, isn't so obvious, but it has to do with the authenticity of the communication.

There are two ways in which we communicate our experience. The first is presentational, which is poetical and non-explanatory. It might be in words, but it might also be a laugh, a cry, a furrowed brow, or even a momentary averting of the eyes. We're acutely sensitive to non-verbal messages from others and tend to react to these in a gut-level manner that's largely unconscious and emotional. The second mode is discursive, which is, by contrast, prosaic and explanatory, and it necessarily engages our logical and discursive minds. Discursive communication is the story or explanation of what we think and how we feel. It's a picture painted in words.

Good actors know how to present themselves in a convincing manner so their presentational and discursive communications are in synch. The result is satisfying for an audience. We enjoy watching them, and we're taken in by the story.

When these two modes of communication are at odds with each other, however, we experience the communication of the other as inauthentic, and this experience is distinctly unsettling. Suppose we're listening to someone whose brow is furrowed tightly, who's periodically clenching their jaw, and whose whole manner appears to be tense and angry. If what they say is, "My mother is a wonderful person," we experience a certain degree of frustration because the words and tone of the words is inconsistent with the facial expression. We haven't received an authentic or complete communication, and we're not convinced.

Authenticity is also the condition in which the outer presentation of a person to another corresponds to their inner experience. In other words, we can say they're being "real." They're honestly presenting externally what they're thinking, feeling, and sensing inside. They're being genuine. When they say they're sad, they're truly feeling sad, and, not only that, but they're presenting being in sadness. When they say they're excited, they don't just say the words, "I'm excited" descriptively, they also act excited.

The authenticity factor is extremely important in the co-evolution process. For us to come to self-awareness, we need to be in touch with the truth of ourselves and tell the truth. To hide, avoid, cover up, or tell a lie only reinforces the illusion we're trapped in. Phony relating doesn't produce real insights. To know the truth, we need to tell the truth. This is the deal that reality has made with us. Unfortunately, many of us miss it. It's one of the central challenges that we all face in life: being true to ourselves, being who we are around others, and feeling okay about being real. The cultivation of authenticity is an important factor.

So, how do we improve the quantity and quality of relating?

Here's what we do. We create the co-evolutionary universe in microcosmic form, structure the relating, and add in agreements that facilitate the quantity and quality of relating with an understanding of what hinders and enhances the process. That's a mouthful, so let's go into the method itself. This method is called the dyad, and I've been using it in my work for over 30 years.

THE DYAD STRUCTURE

The Universe in Microcosm

Because we know co-evolution occurs when one person communicates to another in a communication cycle (sending, receiving, and acknowledgement), we can create a structure that allows for this process to unfold. The basic unit is simple: a listener and a speaker interact without any obtuse esotericism, sacred geometry, or gurus—just a couple of human beings. Dyad means two—in this case, two people. First, we set this up physically, with two individuals sitting directly across from one another a comfortable distance apart, facing and looking at each other. Second, we get the two individuals to agree to certain behavioral procedures and agreements that ensure the completion of the communication cycle.

As we explored in the previous chapter under the section on contact, we need to trust others and ourselves in order to open up to and deepen our contact with them. We need to be assured it will be safe to present who we really are. It's difficult to open up to one another in a chaotic universe if we can't predict how others will treat us when we do open up. Therefore, we need to establish—in advance—our rules of engagement so we know what to expect when we take the risk of expressing the reality of our experience to others.

These agreements and procedures give each person a gradually deepening sense of security and emotional safety so they can go more deeply into their experience and reveal it to the other.

Non-interruption

The first essential agreement is non-interruption. If communication is to be completed, one person must listen, and one person must speak. The two people can't be speaking at the same time. Interruption is the constant bane that breaks down everyday conversation. Sometimes we don't even listen to people; we're just listening for a pause in the other person's sentence so we can get in our two cents' worth. Interruption often accelerates a heated discussion into a fiery argument when people get frustrated and they can't get their point across. If we observed how much interruption occurs, we'd find it amazing that any conversations ever got completed.

So, we need to set up the structure so one person agrees to listen, and the other person agrees to speak—without interruption. We can do this by giving the speaker a limited period of time to speak and then, after this time, the roles change and the listener becomes the speaker and communicates for the same length of time. An optimal period of time is roughly five minutes. This can be done with a stopwatch or a timer that beeps at the end of each interval to indicate the changeover. These alternating five-minute changeovers typically continue for 40 minutes, back and forth.

Confidentiality

The next agreement is common in most self-help groups: confidentiality. We need to concur that whatever is said in the dyad between the two people isn't shared anywhere outside the dyad—not to anyone else, in any other space, under any circumstance... ever. Even the names of the people we shared with shouldn't be mentioned to anyone outside the dyad or outside the group doing dyads.

Non-evaluation

Thirdly, we need to agree that we'll refrain from expressing criticism—either positive or negative, verbally or non-verbally—that's related to what another is presenting or describing. Non-evaluative listening isn't the same as empathetic listening or mirroring, where the listener attempts to ally themselves with the speaker by repeating back to them what they understood. Mirroring takes some skill and, sometimes, the unskilled person can include an unintended judgement that may cause the speaker to shut down The dyad isn't therapy or peer counseling. It's more like an experimental laboratory in which we're creating the best conditions for the emergence of self-insight

The non-evaluation agreement isn't easy to keep, since it's almost entirely foreign to our everyday experience. We may find it extremely difficult, when listening to another, to refrain from making our private judgements. Does what they're saying make sense or not? Do we feel the same way as they do or not? Do we find it interesting or boring? Even when we're listening intently to another, our minds are working overtime.

It's especially important that we try, to the best of our ability, to suspend judgements of another. If that's impossible, we must try our best to avoid communicating our judgements, either verbally or non-verbally. A furrowed brow, a downward tilt of the chin, or a grim set of the mouth may communicate to another that what the speaker is saying isn't acceptable. Their response may be to shut down or cut short their communication. If unconscious behavioural patterns have been triggered, the speaker may do the opposite—communicate reactively to the listener. Either way, the perceived negative evaluation will create a reaction and distract them from open disclosure.

Even if we agree with what a person is saying, it's important to remain neutral. A positive evaluation can subtly reinforce the speaker's false personality instead of opening the space for them to present how they really are. For example, the speaker may think, "They've complimented me on being funny, and I guess they like that, so I won't tell them I'm having a rough time."

Eliminating judgement creates an environment in which the quality of relating or authenticity can be cultivated. Individuals will feel safe to look inside and openly express the truth of themselves freely and honestly.

Non-influence

This agreement is related to the non-evaluation agreement. As listeners, we should avoid trying to help the person find the right words or do anything that assists the person to communicate to us. We should just listen and not speak. It's tempting to help a person when they're struggling to find the right words, but this struggle is actually helping them develop their ability to make the associations of inner experience with language so they can improve their ability to communicate to others in life. If we help them, they're denied the valuable opportunity to evolve this capacity. As listeners, we should also avoid nodding, smiling. or laughing. This eliminates the often-subtle cues that socialize us to be a certain way. By nodding or smiling, we're non-verbally saying to the speaker, "I like what you're saying… say more" or "Be the way I'm liking you to be right now." This body language prevents the person from looking inside to find their own personal truth rather than conform to what the listener likes. Some people will find the avoidance of nodding or smiling difficult—even thinking it's impolite—but when we understand how we unconsciously manipulate each other to be nice or sociable through these habitual subtle cues, we can offer this gift of non-influence to others. When we're on the receiving end of someone just listening, without responding, we experience the wonderful gift of time, within the presence of another, to look inside and find out what's true for us rather than what's true for others. For some people, this is a revolution in their life—to be allowed, for the first time, to go into the inner sanctum of themselves and have a glimpse of their real essence.

Full Attention

Because the evolution of self-awareness evolves through mutual understanding, it's crucially important that we, as listeners, try to fully understand what the person is saying. We should be in a space of non-judgemental openness to what the speaker is presenting. Our main intention is to fully understand what the speaker is communicating.

We should put our full attention on the speaking partner, even if the person speaking closes their eyes to silently contemplate for a while. We should maintain eye contact with the person at all times, whether the person is talking or silent. We should try to avoid being distracted by our own thoughts while we're listening, so we can be fully present for our partner. This is difficult, since people commonly have unrelated thoughts when other people are talking, so we need not be discouraged when we space out or lose concentration. If this happens, we can simply say to our partner, "Say that again," or "Say that again louder" if we missed a phrase or two, or "Summarize that." if the person has said a lot, and we aren't sure about the essence of what the person was trying to say. We, as listeners, could also say, "Clarify _____," adding the sentence or terminology that we didn't understand. These simple instructions can vastly improve the chances of communication getting completed.

At the end of the timed period of five minutes, when the beeper or bell from the timer goes off, as listeners, we say a simple "Thank you" to indicate that we've understood.

This form of full listening has a powerful effect on the speaker. When we listen in this manner, we're adding the energy of our attention to the speaker's attention energy. This provides them with more energy to go within and contemplate their inner dimension. They'll be able to touch their subtler inner realm more clearly with that extra energy. Our attention, in addition, helps keep them on track with their own inquiry, because the speaker knows we're there waiting for a communication from them—unlike in solitary meditation, for example, where beginning meditators can spend 70%-80% of their time spacing out and losing track of their object of concentration.

Full attention is also powerful in the sense that it non-verbally communicates to the speaker, "I care," "I have a regard for you," and "I have compassion for you." Within the warmth of that open space of non-judgement, non-interference, non-interruption, and confidentiality, we can allow ourselves and others to gradually let down their defenses, be more authentic, and say what's been true for many years but has never been said and received by another. There's great potential to let go of the suspended communications and the frozen suffering that has held us back in life, allowing profound healing and insights to occur.

This caring contact is similar in quality to the contact we may experience or search for in a guru. As we do more and more dyads with the same person or different people, we experience the same divine rapport and connection that we look for in the spiritual teacher. And, if we think about this, why shouldn't we? Do we all not arise from the same divine source as a realized teacher? However, in this situation, we're allowing ourselves to be each other's guru. As I said earlier, the saviour is us.

Self-referencing

There are also important agreements we need to follow when it's our turn to speak. To make communication more genuine and authentic, we need to confine it to our personal experience, for that's the only experience about which we can claim any direct knowledge. Sometimes in a conversation, we use the generic form of "you." For example, one might say, "You know when you go to the store, and you have to choose between two types of lettuce, and you can't decide, and you just feel so stupid?" This is a way of speaking about us, or people in general, in a theoretical way. When we speak in this general way, we can run the risk of our partner sitting across from us thinking we're talking about them and feeling evaluated. There can be some confusion in the listener's mind about whether we're referring to them or not. "Is he/she thinking I'm stupid?" This confusion can remain suspended in the mind and be a source of upset if the listener takes it personally. It's much better for each of us, as the speaker, to own what we're saying and refer to ourselves using "I" statements; e.g., "When I go to the store, I sometimes have a hard time making a choice between two types of lettuce, and I feel stupid." This is noticeably clearer with no possible reference to the partner. Use of the universal "we" is okay—as in, "We all want love"—but a person should distinguish if the reference is really about them—"I want love"—and own that. Self-referencing creates an environment of greater authenticity and truthfulness in which people are speaking more from their real self. When this quality of relating or authenticity is enhanced, co-evolution is enhanced as well.

Another aspect of self-referencing is to avoid referring to what your partner said when it's your turn to speak. There's an element of resonance that occurs as people share more intimately their inner landscape with one another. We may see a likeness of another to ourselves as they speak about a life experience. We may have an *aha* moment as they talk about themselves and then, all of a sudden, we have an important insight about our own life situation. The temptation is to say something like, "Wow, I totally relate to what you said. God, I have such a hard time choosing what lettuce to buy and, like you, I feel stupid." We should avoid referring to our partner—especially in the way of making comparisons or offering similarities or differences. To do this runs the risk, once again, of offering an unintended evaluation that could be upsetting or even devastating to our partner. It's much better to let go of what the speaking partner just said in their turn, and be silent, contemplate the subject of our interest, and come up with some insight about ourselves. If what surfaces does relate to what our partner said, when it's our turn to speak, we should phrase it as originating in ourselves, in our own words, in the way that's uniquely our experience. "You know, there are times when I go to the Farmers'

Market, and I just get overwhelmed with all the choices. It reminds me of how overwhelmed I often feel in my life. There are just too many decisions. I wish the world would stop."

As we engage in the dyad with these agreements, there will be a short adjustment period, because the format is different from usual relating. We should realize that this has a different purpose than social conversation, peer support, or counseling. Our goal isn't to get along, have fun, entertain, convince, or help one another, although these are all worthy endeavours. The goal of the dyad exercise is to enhance communication so we can help each other to evolve. The aim is also insight. Once we experience the power of this profound process, we experience the deep fulfillment of mutual understanding and self-awareness.

> *"A mind that conforms to any pattern of authority, inward or outward, cannot be sensitive. It is only when a mind is really sensitive, alert, aware of all its own happenings, responses, thoughts, when it is no longer becoming, no longer shaping itself to be something, only then is it capable of receiving truth. It is only then there can be happiness, for happiness is not an end—it is the result of reality."*
>
> — J. Krishnamurti

PREPARATION BEFORE THE DYAD BEGINS

Now that the physical and non-physical structure is set-up, the communication process can proceed. It's best to begin with a topic or focus that we can inquire into.

Before the communication starts, we should choose something we want to investigate rather than just communicating random thoughts on any subject. We don't all have to choose the same subject. These subjects could be about gaining personal insights—e.g., how we want to be loved, problem resolution, clarifying concepts ("What's a guru?")

or working toward awakening ("Who am I?" or "What's life?"). A list of the subjects of inquiry is provided at the end of this book. It's best that we choose a subject that's of interest to us, since that sense of interest will empower our inquiry. So, we choose an area related to self, life, or another, and then tell the other—our partner in the dyad—what that topic is. (Sometimes there could be two or three subjects of inquiry, as indicated in the exercise portion of the book.)

The questions are phrased in terms of an instruction such as, "Tell me who you are," or, "Tell me some concerns you have about being yourself around others." An instruction is much better than a question such as, "Who are you?" It gives a directive to the mind and indicates what we should do. "Who are you?" doesn't elicit such a response. An instruction does. There's a qualitative difference between a question and an instruction. If the inquiry is put into question form—e.g. "Who are you?"—there's no directive to speak and, in some instances, the question can feel mildly intrusive or confrontational. An instruction is more neutral. The question should be put into an instructional form and then given to the partner.

Once we understand what our respective instructions are, we let our partners know our instruction(s) and decide who's to receive the requests first. We're now ready to start the dyad.

THE CO-EVOLUTION PROCESS WITH DYADS

People who are doing a 40-minute dyad with each other should, first of all, have in place a means of marking off successive five-minute periods, either through the use of a timer or a CD that denotes the eight, five-minute periods with a gong or other sound.

Step 1: Instruction

The listener gives the speaker their instruction in the "Tell me..." format. The "tell me" form is superior to a question, as it requests that the speaker communicate. A question doesn't instruct the speaker to communicate. The wording of the instruction should stay the same as it's repeated without any insertions or additions. In the case of self-inquiry, the listener shouldn't say, "So, um, tell me who you are," and they shouldn't say, "Charles, please tell me who you are." They should simply say, "Tell me who you are" as one uninterrupted thought with no emphasis on any one word. The instruction needs to be given directly to the speaker clearly in a neutral manner without any personality or added emotional nuance.

Step 2: Reception:

The speaker should receive the request as fully as possible, allowing the request to settle into themselves, into their being, in such a way that it can automatically initiate their contemplation.

Step 3: Listening

The listener then places their silent undivided attention on the speaker and watches, listens, and tries to understand without distracting the speaker by nodding or commenting in any way. They should maintain this quality of attention even when their partner is silently contemplating with eyes closed or open. If thoughts or judgements about what's said occur, the listener is to set them aside.

Step 4: Object

Once the speaker receives the request, they should go into silence and get a felt sense of the object or subject they're investigating in the moment.

For example, if the instruction is, "Tell me who you are," what's most real about the self at that moment might be an ache in the lower back. It might be a memory of a time with Grandpa at the beach. It might be a feeling of tiredness or boredom. It might be a thought, such as, "I wonder what's for lunch.". Whatever is most real, most present, in relation to the instruction received is taken as the object of inquiry.

If the instruction is, "Tell me what life is," the person is to direct their attention to their most real experience of life at that moment. It might be the hearing of a bird call. It might be their awareness of someone in the room talking. It might be a memory of seeing Uncle Rocky in his coffin. Whatever is most real, most present, in relation to the instruction received is taken as the object of inquiry.

Similarly, if the request is, "Tell me a problem you're having," they should get a sense of how that problem is experienced in their body.

In this way, the speaker begins with real phenomena rather than an idea or concept, and they avoid getting stuck in their head.

Step 5: Intention

The speaker then sets out to experience the truth of what they're investigating which is to know the essence of what they are inquiring into. They should intend to achieve a deep "knowingness" of what it is they're investigating. If it's a subject of a new understanding, they want to have deep insight into it. If they want to awaken to their true nature, they set out to have a direct experience of their true nature. There's no effort in this step other than a mental decision that insight or awakening will happen even though they don't know how or when it will occur.

Step 6: Contemplation

The speaker then allows him/herself to be open to whatever enters their consciousness that's the result of the intention. "Openness" is a broad term that's often defined by what it isn't. It's a space of non-judgement of what enters the mind. One doesn't try to make anything enter or resist what's coming up in the mind. One doesn't try to force perceptions, thoughts, or feelings to arise or, conversely, manipulate them to leave the mind. It's a space of allowing and a willingness to be surprised by anything that enters into consciousness. What may come up may appear to have nothing to do with the inquiry, and this should be accepted. The speaker should trust that what came up in the contemplation, whether it seems related to the subject or not, has some inner rationale for arising. The person should avoid speaking right away when material shows up and, instead, should sit in silence a while longer as a way of gathering the essence of what occurred.

Step 7: Communication

After the period of contemplation, the speaker is then to find the words necessary to communicate as accurately as possible what arose in their silent contemplation resulting from their intention to experience the truth. It might be helpful to think of "presenting" the contents of their experience to the listener rather than "describing" or "explaining" them. The speaker should use whatever channels of communication they can to get themselves across—words, body language, voice inflection, actions, feelings, etc.—so the listener can fully understand what the speaker experienced. In other words, they should try to be authentic, having the presentation match as closely as possible their experience in the silent contemplation without adding or taking anything away. If there's laughter, sadness, confusion, doubt, dullness, irritation, calmness, excitement, equanimity, etc., the speaker should be in the experience of it and communicate it so the listening partner can understand it fully. Of course, the speaker needs to follow the agreements we discussed above about non-evaluation and self-referencing.

If, at any time, the listener doesn't understand something the speaker has said, he/she can use the communication aids described above: "Clarify ______," "Say that again," or "Summarize that." The listener then says, "Thank you," and the speaker continues with their contemplation/communication. If the five-minute timer hasn't sounded, and the communication is completed, the speaker goes back to Step 2 and contemplates their request again until the five-minute timer goes off.

When the speaker feels they've completed their communication, they put their hand on their heart to indicate this to the listener.

Step 8: Acknowledgement

The listening partner then says, "Thank you," acknowledging the speaker for his or her response to the original instruction. The listener goes back to Step 1 and gives the same instruction again or the next instruction in the series of instructions. The speaker then proceeds through Steps 4 to 7 again.

When the timer sounds at the end of the five-minute period, the speaker wraps up what they're saying and stops speaking. The listening partner then says, "Thank you," once again as an acknowledgement of understanding all that the speaker has communicated.

Some topics of inquiry have two or three instructions and present a different challenge to the speaker. The goal is to cover the two or three parts of the subject within the five-minute period, so the speaker will have to time themselves to a certain extent. If they've covered the two or three parts of the subject and they still have time, they'll receive the first instruction in the series again and contemplate and communicate anything further that comes into their experience.

Step 9: Change-over

When the five–minute timer sounds, the listener says, "Thank you" to the speaker, the roles reverse, and the partners start again. (The speaker becomes the listener and the listener becomes the speaker) proceeding through Steps 1 to 9 until the end of the 40-minute period. As the speakers in each five-minute period encounter their instructions again, they go deeper and deeper into the their inquiry, and important insights occur.

Summary

What we've essentially done with this dyad method is take the natural dynamic of co-evolution already occurring in life and refined it by removing the elements that hinder self-awareness and enhance the elements that increase it. With the agreements of non-interruption, non-evaluation/confidentiality, self-referencing, non-influence, and full attention, we reduce the chances of emotional injury and cultivate an environment where the quality of authenticity or truthfulness of sharing can grow. By structuring the exchange in a "communication cycle," the quantity of relating is increased. People feel safer to share in a deeper, more meaningful way. The open, inviting contact of the listening partner reproduces, in a unique way, the rapport we feel with a guru without having to have a guru. Suspended communications and experiences are completed, and profound healing, deep insights and spiritual experiences can occur in a truly short period of time for those that practice this technique consistently over a number of days. All of this happens in harmony with the way life actually works. Through this method, the aim of ourselves to evolve in consciousness and ability is fulfilled in an ongoing way.

Imagine the possible outcome of individuals agreeing to do the co-evolution process in the dyad format over one to four days. The growth in self and life awareness can be quite remarkable. All of this is without the dogmatic influence of the guru. In fact, you and I become our own gurus.

Here are reports from some of the participants in co-evolution retreats I've led:

> *"I discovered a bond linking myself with others, that we are all beings trapped within our minds trying to communicate our fears and need for love. I am becoming more loving, more real, more open, truthful and trustworthy."*
>
> — Doug Tyler, real estate rep, Toronto, Ontario.

> *"I felt like I accessed the eternal, underlying, universal oneness that we all belong to and create. Half-way through the weekend I found myself sighing a lot. These were not sighs of stress but sighs of bliss. It was my body's way of saying how yummy, this is sooo delightful, peaceful, and wonderful. The dyad technique*

is truly the best gift one could give and receive because they're getting themselves. I recommend it to anyone who has a desire to learn more about themselves and life here on earth."

— Lise Gillis, employment counselor, Kingston, Ontario

"I've learned that the greatest gift I can give to others is myself, to give from who I am and not from some false personality or ego."

— Steven Kovacs, lighting sales, Toronto, Ontario

"It's like I did five years of meditation in one weekend!"

— Beth Clark, yoga and meditation teacher, Kingston, Ontario.

One of the most unique applications of the co-evolution process is a retreat called the Enlightenment Intensive (aka the Coming Home Retreat). Relatively unknown in the West (even though it's existed since 1968), it's consistently helped people achieve deep states of awakening in one and a half to four days. To many, the idea that awakening can occur in this short period may seem unbelievable or even a hoax. For centuries, this process of awakening has typically taken months or years or even a lifetime through extended periods of solitary meditation. However, if we consider that there's been advancement in so many other areas of life–technology, medicine, astronomy, transportation, etc.–it's certainly conceivable that improvements can be made to speed up the process of spiritual growth.

Since most individuals in our Western, busy lifestyle don't have the time to take weeks or months to spend in silence, the co-evolution method and the Enlightenment Intensive makes the prospect of awakening and the benefit of a deeper, more fulfilled life available to a much broader population. Let's explore this method.

Chapter 13

THE ENLIGHTENMENT INTENSIVE

(AKA THE COMING HOME RETREAT)

Ever since humankind became self-aware, we've sought the answers to explain and understand our existence. Does life have a purpose, or is it just a meaningless series of events randomly strung together? Do we, as individuals, actually exist, or are we just part of a dream that someone else is imagining? Do we have a soul or a spirit? Do we exist just for this life or for eternity? Who are we? Is there a real self inside, or are we just a personality that's the consequence of all the developmental influences of our upbringing, culture, peer group, etc.?

Many religions, superstitions, and philosophies have been formed to answer these questions. For most of the world's population, these explanations have been enough, and people are satisfied to not dig any deeper. But a growing number of people are beginning to realize that these explanations are only intellectual understandings and second-hand beliefs. Many of us long to experience the truth directly for ourselves rather than be satisfied with someone else's articulation of what self and life actually are.

Some of us have experienced a degree of suffering in the world or have become disillusioned or disheartened with our existence. As a result, we've been motivated to relieve our suffering by seeking to make sense of our lives and understand if there's a deeper experience of self and a more fulfilled way of living.

Some of us have moved into a path of yearning for more spiritual experience in our lives as a result of our own natural unfoldment. Others of us have tried and tried, using many methods of awakening, and haven't fully succeeded. Some of us may feel ready to give up the search but can't because something deep inside keeps urging us to go on.

Whatever category we fit into, the Enlightenment Intensive gives us an opportunity to finally become successful in the long search for self-realization without the impediment of a dogma. Through this method, we can truly find the guru within.

WHAT IS AN ENLIGHTENMENT INTENSIVE?

The Enlightenment Intensive (aka the Coming Home Retreat) is a four-day retreat that usually begins with supper around 6:30 pm on a Wednesday evening and ends after lunch at 2 pm on Sunday. On Wednesday evening, participants become familiar with each other, the staff, the format, the agreements, the environment, and the technique used on the intensive. Thursday, Friday, and Saturday form the main body of the retreat. Sunday is an integration period in which participants are guided to bring the benefits of the retreat into their lives. The retreat is typically conducted in a rural, secluded environment. All participants stay and sleep at the facility for the duration of the retreat. Meals are organic (when possible) and vegetarian.

Purpose

The retreat provides individuals with the optimal opportunity to awaken to the true nature of self, life, and others. In the process, minor or major barriers to one's deeper fulfillment in life can be dissolved, so that individuals can engage more fully in all of life's experiences with a deeper connection to themselves and others.

History

In the 1950s, Charles Berner, an American spiritual teacher (1929–2007) located in California, had a powerful awakening experience of the co-evolutionary principle of life and saw that, in our true natures, we're all trying to get closer to one another to fulfill our eternal relationship. He formed the Institute of Ability in California and began researching and developing methods following this principle to help people grow personally.

He set out to enhance people's relating ability to improve their lives. When people made agreements of non-interruption, non-evaluation, and listener empathy and agreed only to self-reference rather than discuss what other people said, he found that people became more honest, authentic, and real. In his initial work, he also noticed that the greatest barrier to personal growth occurred as the result of incorrect relating. He saw that, if previous communication with others was injurious, overwhelming, not understood, or incomplete—for example, through difficult childhood experiences—these experiences and the unfulfilled communications were suspended in the mind, creating an unconscious reactivity. When people encountered present situations similar to those that took place in the past, these old experiences were triggered. This reactivity was the primary source of problems in life.

A major part of his work was the development of the dyad technique, where partners would take turns as the listener and the speaking partner, asking each other many questions and relating within communication guidelines. They were able to complete past unresolved communications and, as a result, they became more problem-free, mentally and emotionally balanced, more alive and engaged, and their life worked better.

The Addition of Inquiry

Then in 1968, it occurred to Charles after reading Philip Kapleau's book, *The Three Pillars of Zen,* that the dyad format, which had worked so well in other areas of his work, might be used to answer life's most important questions.

Charles and his wife, Ava, gathered their students together and added an inquiry step to the process in which the speaking partner would receive the request, "Tell me who you are." The speaker would then go into a meditative silence, put their attention on themselves, and intend to directly experience their true nature. They'd then communicate what they came up with to the listening partner as they usually did in the dyad structure.

They were surprised and amazed to find that, within a period of just a few days, the students were having enlightenment experiences. They realized soon after they'd taken the best of the Eastern technique of Zen inquiry and added it to the Western technique of relational psychology and that a powerful synthesis of the Eastern and Western approaches to personal evolution took place. They not only discovered a method to bring people to enlightenment in a short period of time but also a way to help people clear the reactive mind of minor or major barriers. Charles and Ava further refined the format over about 50 intensives until they felt they had the final form.

The four-day format was optimal. Anything less didn't allow enough time for the emptying of the mind and the deepening of awakening through the communication part of the technique. They called the retreat the Enlightenment Intensive. I lead the same retreat under the name, the Coming Home Retreat.

WHAT IS ENLIGHTENMENT?

Although enlightenment has had many names throughout history depending on the tradition, and there are many opinions of what the phenomenon is, this is the understanding of enlightenment as it occurs on the retreat: **Enlightenment is the direct experience of the true nature of self, life, or others.**

"Direct experience," as we explored earlier, is beyond all the indirect methods we commonly depend on for knowing, such as sensing, thinking, learning, deciding, reasoning, or feeling. It's beyond intellectual understanding and belief.

Direct experience also means to be in union. For a brief moment in time, we're no longer separated from our true essence. We're united. The seeker and the sought are the same. We're one with ourselves. We're "real-I-zed".

"True nature" encompasses the essence of who we are and what life and others are beyond the mind, emotions, and body—what we were born as before all the influences of personal history and before the ego was formed by the socialization of family, friends, school, job, culture, and society and the developmental influences of pain, trauma, and abuse.

With direct experience, we unite with our true nature in a timeless instant, a spontaneous, "aha" flash, that lights up our whole being in such a way that we experience the magnificence of the true self but also know it with absolute certainty and without doubt. The awareness is self-evident. As a result, we drop more of the false personality that we've been trapped in and come home to the authentic, natural self. We're more able to present ourselves from this state. It's a simple, exhilarating, revitalizing, life-altering spiritual experience accompanied by a deep sense of peace, serenity, bliss, and inner harmony.

THE CO-EVOLUTION PROCESS IN THE ENLIGHTENMENT INTENSIVE

The main technique practiced in the Intensive, as mentioned earlier, is the dyad: the structured form of partner-assisted meditation in which two people sit across from one another to contemplate and communicate. During the retreat, each participant first selects and focuses on one of five fundamental questions: Who am I? What am I? What is Life? What is Another? What is Love?

Ten to 12 times a day, participants choose a different partner and sit across from each other on a pillow or a chair at a comfortable distance apart. During each 40-minute dyad, the two partners take five-minute turns being the contemplator/communicator or the attentive listener. The instructions are simple: set about to experience directly the essential truth underlying the question, and then tell the partner whatever occurs.

This is all done in a supportive environment under the guidance of an experienced facilitator and staff. No religious or philosophic belief system is taught. The workshop leader is only a facilitator. He/she doesn't tell participants what to believe and only gives instructions on the technique to guide individuals through any difficulties that occur as they do it.

The Guidelines

During an Enlightenment Intensive retreat, participants are asked to honour a number of guidelines. These agreements support the emotional safety, focus, and effectiveness of the retreat. Participants agree to:

- Eat, sleep, and stay at the site during the intensive.
- Keep confidential anything said by others.
- Refrain from evaluating fellow participants.
- Take care of all outside concerns before the Intensive, and allow any non-essential messages to be handled by the retreat staff, except for emergencies.
- Eat only the food and snacks served.
- Avoid smoking, illegal drugs, alcohol, or caffeinated beverages. (It's suggested to refrain from these for a week prior to the retreat to avoid withdrawal symptoms.)

- Leave adornments such as jewelry, makeup, perfume, cologne, and other scented products at home or in the car. Non-scented deodorant is acceptable.
- Keep at home or in the car anything that may become a distraction such as books, magazines, journals, radio, cellular phone, or laptop.
- Refrain from all sexual activity.
- Put aside all other practices, and put all effort into using only the techniques taught during the Intensive.
- Observe silence outside the dyad sessions.

The Schedule

The schedule is similar to but not exactly the same as many typical meditation retreats. After the orientation evening on Wednesday, participants begin the day on Thursday, Friday, and Saturday at 6 am and continue until approximately 10:30 pm with an hour of rest in the afternoon. The day is structured with dyads interspersed with meals, snacks, outside walks, exercise, talks, and silent sitting. Sunday is an integration day that ends around 2 pm.

Is It Really Possible to Get Enlightened in One and a Half to Four Days?

One of the biggest barriers to awakening (and to people attending the retreat) is the belief that awakening cannot occur in one and a half to four days. The assumption is that it must take a lot longer. This may be the case in other traditional forms of meditation but not for the Enlightenment Intensive. In the 60 years since Enlightenment Intensives began, there has been confirmation from thousands of people all over the world that the same experience that people have attained using other forms of self-inquiry or meditation—which take from two weeks to 10 years—occurs in the Intensive. A significant percentage of participants succeed in this time. Experienced truth seekers who've found difficulty in the past with other methods may find all their previous attempts rewarded during this concentrated effort.

Those new to self-inquiry often find it easier than veteran seekers who may have to overcome their own expectations and preconceived ideas of what the awakening experience is. Many report having enlightenment experiences on the way home or in the days or weeks following the intensive.

THE STEPS LEADING TO ENLIGHTENMENT

There are eight steps or stages that people pass through during the Enlightenment Intensive retreat on the way to having a direct experience. Participants may go through some or all of these stages, or they may spend a lot or a little time in each stage and return to previous stages or jump ahead a stage.

1. Giving Answers

One gives their partner answers that are already known. These have been learned from parents, teachers, clergy, and friends. They may have been acquired in books or from other teachers. By presenting these answers to partners, they're cleared from the mind.

2. Intellectualizing

One thinks things out logically and reasonably; e.g., "If this is true, then that must be true," and so on. Sometimes in this stage, one may come upon the so-called correct answer. But answers—correct or not—aren't what one is looking for. This stage is finished when one stops trying to answer a question and begins to set about to experience reality directly.

3. Phenomena

One may have been overusing the brain to such a degree that it may begin to produce unfamiliar mental and physical phenomena. Visions may appear. The room may appear to distort. One may see auras around people and things. One may experience hot and cold flashes or waves of emotion running through the body. Not everyone experiences these, but once the phenomena are communicated to a listening partner in the dyad, they disappear.

4. The Void

One may find the field of consciousness empty. No thoughts occur, and no progress appears to be made. At this stage, one stops trying to make awakening happen by looking for the self and instead surrenders more to the experience in the moment, allowing the direct experience to occur in greater openness.

The distinction between looking for something and allowing enlightenment to happen may seem subtle, but it makes all the difference in the world. This stage is also known as the quieted mind and is often the end goal of many schools of meditation. However in the retreat, participants are encouraged to not be seduced by and stop in this phase of serenity and calmness, but to continue on their inquiry.

5. Emotions

One may have feelings of fear, anger, grief, sadness, apathy, or the opposite—bliss and serenity—as one experiences and communicates the emotional sense of self, which has been confused with the true self. Feelings of fear may arise when one de-identifies or separates the true self from these mental-emotional ego states. The key to moving through these barriers is one's willingness to communicate these feelings and experience whatever it takes to find the truth.

6. The Enlightenment Experience

If the participant is graced by enlightenment, two things occur simultaneously. One will have a direct, conscious experience of self while experiencing a release of energy. The direct experience occurs in a timeless instant and will be known as a definite breakthrough.

There will be no doubt. One may cry in gratitude, experience ecstasy, or laugh uproariously at the obviousness of who they actually are.

7. The Glow

The energy that's been trapped by holding onto the false sense of self (the ego) is released, and one's presence will radiate as one stays in union with their true self. This will continue until the direct experience has been fully presented to others.

8. The Pure Steady State

Once the energy is discharged and one spends time fully communicating the direct experience to partners, one will move into a steady state of being present in the true self and be in contact with it directly. The steady state will continue to the degree that one continues to present their true self to others in life and engage in spiritual practices.

THE VALUE OF ENLIGHTENMENT IN LIFE

We can take any workshop on success psychology or on how to be more effective in achieving and manifesting our goals, and, to a certain degree, we'll be happy. However, if we don't know who it is that's succeeded, we'll have failed at being fulfilled in life. We'll have become a successful failure. History is full of successful people who, at the end of their lives, grieve because they didn't find true happiness. The tragedy isn't that they died but that they didn't truly live. They may have certainly reached all their goals but may not have fully engaged in life because they didn't know what life really was and, therefore, didn't fully engage with it. They may not have fully lived in life because they didn't know who it was that wanted to live. They missed the point of life while some other personality was occupying their existence!

Similarly, many of us live in accordance with what we think life is and who we think we are. The important point is…we only *think* we know. We're living from an intellectual concept that's been programmed over time by the family and culture in which we grew up. It's as if we're all actors born and raised on a stage, taking our cues and roles from all the older actors. We gain acceptance of our behaviour from others and think this acceptance verifies that our self-image is who we are. It's not. It's just a reinforced socialized personality. We're unconsciously stuck in it, thinking that others' ideas of who we are is actually who we are. We suffer out of our own unconsciousness, not really knowing why we suffer.

When we live from a personality, we live in a reduced state of experience. The personality is, in reality, a false identity state that's created from a belief about ourselves and life and others: "I'm no good", "I'm unlovable," "I don't exist," "I'm not important," or, "Life is too hard," "You can't trust others," "Love hurts." Every experience we have is filtered through this personality and accepts or rejects the life experience that reinforces the belief. We only see what we believe, and we reject the rest. The false belief is, in reality, superimposed onto us, and we act according to this belief and continue to re-create the same suffering.

There are thousands of seminars and techniques that propose the remedy to all of this is to just change your beliefs. "Change your beliefs, and change your life"—i.e., to affirm, declare, or even implant in the subconscious through various forms of therapy a positive belief. But this is just like rearranging the chairs on the deck of *The Titanic*. It's superimposing another personality onto the self. It's still a mask.

So, to live from a personality means the energy of life is buffered, existence is experienced selectively only from a single point of view, and we live imprisoned in the walls of our ego. Living from a personality provides some degree of happiness, but we won't find true fulfillment in it. However, if we directly experience who we are—the true self behind the personality, and, in fact, the one who created our personality—the possibility of greater fulfillment in life exists.

The potential is that we can become more engaged in life. We're more available to all experiences. We'll experience joy and also sadness more fully. We'll laugh more and more deeply and, when it's appropriate to cry, we'll cry more deeply. We'll allow our experiences in life to flow through us and be completed rather than blocking them, denying them, or suspending them because of the filtering quality of our ego. We feel more in the flow of our lives.

We'll have more rewarding relationships because we'll be more available to others. Relationships are all about the authenticity of the connection. To truly have a satisfying intimate relationship, it's essential that we know who we and what others are. If we don't know who we're *connecting from* and what we're *connecting to*, we'll only connect to others through the buffer of a false personality. Trying to navigate through the maze of two personalities to truly touch one another when we're not self-realized is impossible.

Because we're more engaged in life, we can take any growth technique or religious practice and make more rapid and ongoing progress with it because we can bring to bear our own personal power of choice to be open and grow. In the success area of life, we can make real progress toward real goals and actually be happy, because our real self is now living our life.

Enlightenment can turn a person on to truth and the actuality of that truth in day-to-day life. We can discover that there's more to life than just gratifying the senses. This whole business of life isn't just some random occurrence with no direction or purpose. We can make these discoveries not as ideas but as living facts. Such discoveries fundamentally alter one's life.

When we comprehend that, basically, we all want to be seen for who we truly are and relate to others authentically, we understand that, on a daily basis as we live from our essential self in real contact with others, this actually uplifts others through the natural dynamic of co-evolution. As a side effect, people in the Intensive gain communication skills almost without realizing it by practicing the co-evolution technique.

Lack of real communication and real listening creates the greatest suffering in life. In an Enlightenment Intensive, individuals can make significant gains in this ability just by participating in the retreat.

In the end, however, the retreat has only one purpose: enlightenment. It's its own reward because it's the fulfillment of life. That union with truth, no matter how brief, is our inherent purpose, and fulfilling that purpose is the greatest benefit gained from an enlightenment experience.

> *"In short, the Enlightenment Intensive is a powerful method, which produces remarkably consistent results. The method has been developed thoroughly, tested all over the world, and participated in by thousands and thousands of people. It is the most effective method for self-discovery that I have ever seen, and it is one that can be used by almost anyone.*
>
> *"It is an amazing development in the field of spiritual growth, to have the awakening project be available to such a large portion of the people in such an accelerated fashion."*
>
> — Charles Berner — originator of the Enlightenment Intensive.

A LIST OF BENEFITS

After an Enlightenment Intensive, participants commonly report feeling:

- More authentic
- Peace, contentment, and lightness permeating their body
- Totally embodied, as if they've finally come home to themselves
- Loving-kindness toward themselves and others
- Greater self-acceptance
- Psychologically whole
- Greater inner strength and resolve

- Freer to express themselves around others
- Improved intuitive ability
- Enhanced and balanced energy levels

Participants also report having greater capacity to:

- Be open and authentic in relationships
- Persist and accomplish personal goals
- Face and overcome problems and difficulties
- Fully experience love, joy, and happiness
- Understand the deeper truths in traditional philosophy and religion
- Naturally and honestly be themselves in relationships
- Be assertive and communicate their needs
- Find meaning, inspiration, and insight
- Make rapid progress in their personal and spiritual growth

TESTIMONIALS: WHAT FORMER PARTICIPANTS HAVE SAID ABOUT ENLIGHTENMENT INTENSIVES (AKA THE COMING HOME RETREAT)

"Enlightenment Intensives are very pure and powerful. The value they had for me I can't say enough about. Enlightenment made apparent to me what my mind is and what I am and I became conscious of what others actually are. As a result, my approach to Martial Arts completely transformed and my ability improved dramatically. I highly recommend Enlightenment Intensives to anyone."

— Peter Ralston, California, first non-Asian ever to win a World Championship Tournament of Martial Arts (1978, Republic of China)

"When I am in union with myself, sounds are as if inside my body, voices vibrate in my chest, colors are bright and clear, my love comes out without holding back; I speak the truth clearly from deep inside me—totally satisfying and pleasurable. My face and eyes look straight at others; I am relaxed. Nothing in me wants to hide. There is no judgment, of others or myself. My breath flows clearly as if to my toes with no congestion, because there is no congestion in my mind—because there is no mind.

"I occupy every part of my body—nothing can hurt me. I feel complete, wanting for nothing. I am gentle, at one with others. I could not hurt them. I know their thoughts. I do not think to do anything; it is done. There is no space, no delay between my actions and me. I am appropriate, balanced. Ecstasy flows through my body and being like waves. I feel humble, grateful for this state of grace. The truth has set me free..."

— Osha Reader, Director of Origin Retreat Center, California

". . . Over and over I am asked, 'Tell me who you are.' Each time. . . I turn inward and focus my intent on directly experiencing the 'I am' that is beyond thought, word and action. Letting go of what I anticipate the experience to be, my body begins to move. My back arches on an inhale, my shoulders are thrown back and my face turns up toward the sky with a long sigh that builds to a low moan on the exhale. My muscles tense and relax in an undulating rhythm. Each time I go into myself, the movement is more intense, my breath deeper and faster. I had expected some kind of serene peace or sense of all-encompassing benevolence, an infinite stillness—not this heat, this surge of power, this explosion of sensation and movement in my body. Gradually I stop

worrying about what others might think and open more and more to the direct experience.

"It's like riding a dragon through the night sky. I feel the fire that is myself and more than me, and I ride the flame. The boundaries between myself and the walls of the room, the floor beneath me, the person across from me, the trees outside dissolve in the heat. All the edges are ash. There is nothing that is not dragon-winged with feathers of turquoise, vermillion, azure. For a moment I am afraid it will tear me open—and it does—and I am the dragon. The joy of no separation fills me, even as the heat continues to sear through me. I am the heat and the searing. Metaphor can only approximate what is beyond words. When I emerged from the Enlightenment Intensive . . . all of my worries about the future and my resentments about past hurts seemed, in that moment, very small when compared to the vastness that is both what I am and the reality in which I participate."

— Oriah Mountain Dreamer, writing of her experience in *The Invitation* by Oriah Mountain Dreamer, copyright 1999; published by Harper ONE, San Francisco. Edited and presented with permission by the author. www.oriah.org

"I have found the practice of the Enlightenment Intensive to be an invaluable experience along the journey of discovery. I more or less stumbled on my first one, not really knowing what I was getting myself into. However, it has had a lasting effect on my daily life. I feel a greater sense of confidence, equanimity and, surprisingly...wonder. The methodology combines a form of Zen koan practice with Western relational psychology, though it is not aligned with any theoretical or philosophical school.

The format is simple and demanding. To discover the truth of ourselves and of existence, we must necessarily move beyond the numerous and ingenious devices we employ to avoid its raw reality. For some people, the search for that truth is the only really meaningful activity of life. I would recommend the practice to anyone who falls into that category."

— Sandra Fiegehen, Ph.D., psychologist, Peterborough

"I recently attended my first Enlightenment Intensive in 2011. As a seasoned traveler of the Way, I can testify that the technique works. As time goes on, I find I'm only interested in what works: this does. During the retreat, my realization was a slow and gradual one– which was exactly my intention. What's more, as the weeks since the retreat have unfolded, I am delightfully surprised to discover that the retreat experience was only the beginning. My awakening process is very active and increasing in depth and clarity. I have happily added the dyad communication technique to my other practices creating a dynamite trio of practice. Thank you, Russell, for keeping this going and offering it to as many people as possible, as well as for your gentle guiding presence!"

— Pat Parisi, counselor, Toronto

"I've never in my entire 50 years been so happy and positive about my life. It's a totally different happiness than the one I used to know. It bubbles up from deep within and explodes through every cell of my body. It's totally awesome. I also, for the very first time in my life, don't worry about the constant approval of others about me. I KNOW WHO I AM and no matter what they say, this is ME and I'm totally happy

with myself and who I am! This is such a breakthrough for me. I've had my downs as well since I left the Intensive, but the downs don't even come close to the highs that I used to have. I have a totally new life! I'm totally out of the dark and dingy prison that I lived throughout all of my life. I've broken the shackles that I created, and I feel totally free! Love and compassion have a totally different meaning and feeling to me. I truly feel that I've got a second chance in life, and it couldn't be any greater and better. I feel so excited that I could burst!"

— Eliane Priese, accountant, Holland Centre, Ontario

"I took my first E.I. in the early '80s, over 20 years ago, and I am still reaping the rewards from that experience. I could not be the person I am today without it. So much so that I encouraged my partner to take last weekend's intensive and, although doubtful, she is now also amazed and has started blossoming like a brand-new flower. I can't say enough about this system of reaching and discovering for the first time your own inner truths and discovering truly what a wondrous being you are. Your whole world will change before your eyes. So, don't hesitate, GO for it. What you will get will be the real you, and you will love it".

— Rudi Colme, artist/designer, Holland Centre, Ontario

"After a day and a half at the seminar, on Saturday morning while I was eating breakfast, it happened. It was as if I had never been here before, I was born again, and everything was a brand-new experience and what an experience it was. I then knew who I was. I knew that I was eternal. It happened just like Russell said. I was eating breakfast on Saturday morning

and, like the snap of the finger, I was awake, the light came on, and I knew who I was. Everything was new, like I had never seen it before, and it was exquisite. I was born again, free to experience life with the knowing that I would never die. The body might go but I would live on."

— Roger Groulx, Ottawa, Ontario

"It (the E.I.) is truly a powerful technique...My, my, my. How does one find the words? The full realization of it (my Enlightenment) did not come until the second to last dyad on the third day. My question was... What Is Life? ... Well...as I try to type the words, to share the experience, I feel myself holding back the words because no words can convey the Sacredness of it... LIFE IS THE FACE OF GOD...

"These words have been parroted a million times by a million tongues, but the truth is ... and this is no metaphor ... LIFE IS THE FACE OF GOD, and I have seen it. It is the very face which I have been searching for my whole life and it is all-pervading, everywhere and ALL There IS... There is nowhere I can be and nothing that I can 'do' that is not BEING in the arms of The Beloved. This very life that I am is that. To experience this is the Divine Union of the Lover and the Beloved, which I have longed for, my whole life, to experience. I did not know ... I do not know... whether I am Loving or being loved... That was/is the predominate feeling coursing through me...LIFE IS THE BELOVED, BEING and the UNION OF IT is WHO I AM and it is so powerful. At the moment of realization ... the words of Rumi shouted in my head: 'From the beginning of my life I have been looking for your face but today I have seen it.'"

— Kamakshi, massage therapist, Michigan

"Had I not attended your EI back in the Spring, I would not now have the unshakeable strength of knowing deeply who and what I am which sustains me on a moment-to-moment basis in a quiet, steadfast, joyful way. I don't know why, nor I can explain it, but I continue to wake up happy every day, thankful every day and smiling at work even though I'm in an impossible situation. Now that can only come from the direct experience I had at your EI and without it I'm sure I'd be discouraged, depressed, muddling through, cranky and grousing like everyone around me. I have more energy now than I have ever had in my life, my husband has been unendingly and enormously supportive and understanding and life is good. Tough, but good. Sometimes life has to slam me up against the wall and let me deal with it so I can discover more of who I really am. So, thank you, Russell, for helping me to see the reality and beauty of life, how I am not separate from all life but am one with all of life and how the Universe supports us on so many levels in so many subtle and very palpable ways."

— Gail Buss, Philadelphia, Pennsylvania

"I really had no idea what to expect when I went to the Enlightenment Intensive, but it was rewarding beyond belief! By the third day, I was sitting in meditation contemplating the question, 'Tell me who you actually are.' I began to notice a strange sensation in the middle of my chest. It was like shutters were trying to open. There was an energy pushing them open from the inside but outside forces kept slamming them shut. But this energy was persistent. It was from my heart. Suddenly the shutters opened wide and stayed open. It was in that instant that I met my spirit. I saw that everything about me was divinely beautiful and infinitely perfect. I knew

that I had always been and would carry on through infinity. I had an image of myself dribbling a basketball and going for a layup on the court. I had no idea if I made the basket because that wasn't the point. The point was that I got to live my life with ME! I got to experience life as myself. Everything, no matter what it was, no matter how magnificent or horrible, was still worth experiencing because I was the one living it and I'm the most precious, miraculous, joyful energy to spend the rest of my life with! I get to be me!!!! And 'me' is exhilarating and sweet.

"I walked up to the retreat guide in the middle of the meditation and I said, 'I have something I want to tell you. I think I have the answer to your question.' He made space for me to sit down and I looked into his eyes and said tremulously, 'I am me!' A tear began to roll down one of his cheeks and a smile spread across his face like a proud father who has just watched his child take his first steps. He nodded his head jubilantly and hugged me warmly. From that moment on I felt like I had been given a new life. Through the rest of the sessions, I was giddy and would frequently break into cartwheels and jump up and down shouting, 'I am me! I am me!!' During the outdoor walking meditations, I remember singing at the top of my lungs, 'I'm singing in the rain!' Even though it was February, and we were in the middle of heavy snowfall, I felt like everything in life was there for me and it was all so beautiful.

"The power of that self-discovery was enormous in my life and it has carried me through many struggles since. The place in my heart that was closed is now open and alive with the knowledge that I am me. There is no need for anything else. I am fulfilled with this gift. And I am thrilled to be me. I don't know how

else I could have ever come to the understanding that I am this infinite, completely perfect spirit. There is nothing more beautiful in life than the recognition of who you actually are!"

— Cheryl Laird, Guelph, Ontario

Enlightenment Intensives (the Coming Home Retreats) aren't an exclusive part of any organization, religious or otherwise. There's nothing to join and no one to follow. The facilitators of Enlightenment Intensives aren't members of any particular organization, religious or otherwise. There are, however, teachers, groups, and schools who've added the Enlightenment Intensive—in whole or in part—to their teachings and practices simply because the technique works.

I personally renamed the intensive the **Coming Home Retreat**. The new name avoids all the confusion, discussions, and different concepts that people have about the word "enlightenment." In addition, "coming home" is very much like the feeling individuals have when they experience who they actually are. Upon awakening, people feel, for the first time, that they truly inhabit their body. There's a deep familiarity with and acceptance of themselves. They feel full and comfortable with an inner sense of belonging in themselves in the here and now. There's a renewed sense of vitality and contentment that blossoms from within as their natural, default state of being.

If you're interested in attending a Coming Home Retreat, my contact information is at the back of the book along with information on how you can contact other facilitators of the retreat in your area.

OUR JOURNEY SO FAR

So, we've come a long way in our journey of awakening and enlightenment. We explored the purpose of a spiritual path, what truth is, and how to experience it. We've looked at methods that don't get us to truth and the power of dogma to trap us, and we understand what insight and awakening actually are. We've examined the characteristics of enlightenment and how to live from that state. We've also investigated the difference between a "dogma" guru and a real spiritual teacher and looked at our responsibility to become a conscious seeker and how to manage dogma. We explored the basic co-evolutionary structure of existence and learned how, by refining this process, can come to deeper insight and even enlightenment through the process of the Enlightenment Intensive. It's been a wonderful exploration together, but it could end up being just another book sitting beside your bed gathering dust from another author presenting more dogma, interesting ideas, and possibilities that made a bit of difference in your life but not a lot.

It could become the kind of book that, years later, you notice on your bookshelf and recall, "Hmm, co-evolution. I can't quite remember what was in that book, but I think it was an interesting idea."

MISSION POSSIBLE

Your task now, should you wish to choose it:

What if this book could make a big difference in your life? **What if you could bypass dogma and become your own guru?** What if this book could bring you solidly into your own unique spirituality through deeper insights and even awakening experiences that transform your life? You may recall that at the beginning of this book I said not to believe anything I say until you, in your own experience, prove it to be so. I also said that at the end of the book, the final word will be yours. Now it's time for you to be the judge. Why not choose to find out if this whole business of co-evolution is true? As with anything, that choice to grow in awareness begins with you. That choice began eons ago in any case, when we decided to become conscious of our divine nature, become separate gods, and relate to each other in a co-evolutionary universe.

Try being in your life now with this new awareness, and keep working on improving your communication skills so you can achieve greater mutual understanding with others and, in so doing, evolve spiritually. Even better, choose to start your own co-evolution group. When you organize a co-evolution group, you create an oasis in life where people can be understood, accepted, authentic, and compassionate with each other. It can be a refuge from a confusing world where individuals who don't feel they fit with any religion or spiritual practice will find a community of liked-minded truth-seekers. Over time, such a group can develop lasting satisfying friendships that bring a deep fulfillment to life that most people yearn for.

It's relatively easy to form a co-evolution group. All you need is yourself, one or more people, and a set of procedures and instructions that I'll provide in the next chapter.

Chapter 14

ORGANIZING A CO-EVOLUTION GROUP

It's relatively easy to form a co-evolution group doing dyads, as the group can consist of two or more people. Here are some suggestions:

Start off by scheduling a period of time of one to three hours to do one or two dyads. (Once you do one or two dyads, you can schedule a day of dyads later if you wish.) This could be in the evening or daytime. Invite people to attend, and explain in advance the concept of co-evolution and how the dyad process works. Have chairs or cushions for enough people, a list of dyad instructions on paper, boxes of Kleenex, a timer that can be set for five-minute intervals, and some snacks/tea for after the session. If available, have one person who's experienced in doing dyads explain the process.

PROCEDURE

1. Start with a brief sharing circle. Have people in the group introduce themselves and briefly say (in one or two minutes) what they're challenged by in their lives right now. (This can be useful for them when selecting the instructions they want to work on.)

2. Read over the guidelines for the group and ask everyone to agree to them. (See Guidelines, below.)
3. Read over or explain the procedure for doing dyads for any newcomers and answer any questions they have. (See the dyad technique for enlightenment and insight below). Sometimes, it's helpful for two people to demonstrate the technique briefly.
4. Have people assemble in the room in pairs sitting directly across (not at an angle) from one another. A good distance between each pair of partners is 18" to 24".
5. Pass out the dyad instruction sheets. (You will find the instructions at the end of this book) Ask people to select a dyad to work on (some dyads have more than one instruction) and tell their partner which instructions they are selecting. Have people choose who will speak first.
6. When people are ready to begin say, "Listening partner, give the instruction. Begin," and start the timer so it goes off every five minutes. The dyad should continue for 40 minutes.
7. At the end of the 40 minutes, each person should take one minute to share with their partner the most important thing they got from the dyad (without referring to anything their partner said).
8. Take a break for 10 minutes.
9. Repeat Steps 5-7.
10. Have people sit in a circle at the end of the meeting and take one minute to share (without referring to anything anyone else said) the most important insight they got from the process.
11. Set up the next meeting and remind people of the confidentiality agreement.
12. Offer snacks and beverages.

(Note: If there are an odd number of people in the group, the organizer can sit out and answer any questions that may occur as new people do the dyads, or three people can do a triad in which they sit in a circle. In this case, two people are listening partners, and the person to the right of the speaking partner gives the instruction to the speaker. At the end of five minutes, the speaker gives the new speaker to his/her left the respective instruction(s) to the new speaking person. In a triad over a 40-minute period, two people will have three times to speak, and one person will have two times to speak.)

GUIDELINES FOR THE CO-EVOLUTION GROUP

To establish a foundation for an open and authentic sharing, attendees are required to agree to these guidelines for participation in the group. Group members agree to:

1. Keep confidential anything that another group member says or does during the duration of the meeting.
2. Avoid evaluating or communicating evaluations or judgements about anything a group member says or does during the meeting.
3. Touch or hug other members only after getting their consent.
4. Avoid commenting on or referring to anything any other group member shares during the co-evolution group.
5. Use "I" statements when sharing personal ideas and understandings, as the listener may perceive" you" statements as a personal comment or evaluation by the speaker.
6. Avoid giving advice to others.
7. Leave a donation to compensate for the costs of running the meeting if required.
8. Place any open beverage cups or glasses with liquid in them to the side of the room or on a table where they won't be accidentally knocked over.

CO-EVOLUTION WITH THE DYAD TECHNIQUE

The co-evolution process helps individuals find greater clarity and greater access to inner truth. It's based on the principle that awareness increases as the result of supportive and authentic relating between two individuals.

Here's summary of the dyad technique as described in Chapter 12:

The Dyad Technique for Enlightenment or Insight

Position: Two individuals, not involved in trying to straighten out their relationship, sitting in a dyad. They decide who will speak and listen first and what instruction(s) they each will work on. It's not necessary that they work on the same instruction.

Step 1. Instruction: The listener gives the speaker their instruction in the "Tell me" form; e.g., "Tell me who you are." "Tell me what life is," "Tell me a problem you're having."

Step 2. Reception: The speaker accepts the instruction and proceeds through Steps 4 to 7

Step 3. Listening: The listener watches, listens, and tries to understand without commenting, nodding, or evaluating in any way.

Step 4. Object: The speaker first gets a real sense, in the moment, of the subject they're working on; e.g., self, life, or a personal issue.

Step 5. Intention: The speaker then intends to experience the truth of the subject they're working on.

Step 6. Contemplation: While holding this intention, the speaker remains open to an experience of the truth of the subject they're inquiring into and anything else that may occur in the mind, emotions, or body as a result of this intention.

Step 7. Communication: The speaker then communicates to the listener whatever occurred as a result of contemplating, trying not to leave anything out or add anything. The speaker tries to keep a balance between silent contemplation and communication. When the speaker completes their communication, they put their hand on their heart.

Step 8. Acknowledgment: The listening partner then says, "Thank you," acknowledging the speaker for his or her response to the original instruction. The listener goes back to Step 1 and gives the same instruction again or the next instruction in the series of instructions.

Step 9. Change-over: When the five-minute timer sounds, the listener says, "Thank you," and the roles reverse. The speaker becomes the listener, and the listener becomes the speaker as they proceed through Steps 1 to 9.

The total time of the dyad is 40 minutes, segmented into eight, five-minute periods of speaking and listening.

Conclusion

In many ways, the co-evolution method using the dyad technique combines the ancient Eastern practice of contemplative meditation and adds the Western method of relating (drawn from modern psychology). The synthesis of both results in a method that's a vast improvement over each one individually. When ultimate questions such as, "Tell me who you are," or "Tell me what life is" are utilized, insights can occur quickly, and awakening can even occur in two to five days. It's estimated that the dyad technique is 50 to 100 times faster at producing enlightenment experiences compared to many traditional forms of meditation. As such, this method is particularly suited to our faster-paced, results-oriented Western culture. The process of co-evolution of consciousness that's naturally occurring already in life—but impaired by the lack of safe rules of engagement—is vastly accelerated.

The dyad technique has established itself as a revolutionary awareness tool in the modern era of human development.

I've included quite a number of dyads on different topics near at the end of this book. Please check them out and give them a try. I guarantee you'll be utterly amazed at the results you receive from them.

Chapter 15

CO-EVOLUTION GROUPS

So far, we've applied the dynamics of Co-evolution to one-on-one relating or dyads, but the dynamics can also be used to accelerate the development of awareness in a group.

RESONANCE

An interesting phenomenon called resonance is accentuated more in a group than it is in one-on-one relating. Resonance happens in music when one note is plucked on a stringed instrument and causes the same note on another stringed instrument to vibrate in sympathy without being plucked. In a similar way, when authenticity is increased and group members are communicating their insights, there's a tendency for others in the group to contact similar truths within themselves. There's a sense of group consciousness that develops in which all members as a team are cooperatively engaged in digging into a great mystery and sharing their realization with one another for the benefit of all. This is a democratic process and refreshingly different from the hierarchical dispensation of truth that's characteristic of traditional religions. Everyone is an equal player yet adds a unique individual perspective that contributes to the collective upliftment of each person in the group. As people communicate and are fully understood without interruption, communication cycles are completed and "aha" experiences and epiphanies become commonplace. People leave the group with greater consciousness of self, life, and others instead of simply contemplating on their own. To allow the fullest participation of all members of the group, these groups are kept to only three to six members.

There are two types of co-evolution groups: **An Insight group and a Truth Group**.

THE CO-EVOLUTION INSIGHT GROUP

The procedure of the Insight group is almost the opposite of the dyad process, yet the end result is the same. In a dyad, we start off with an instruction such as, "Tell me who you are" and end up with a first-hand insight or direct experience that originates from ourselves. In an Insight group, we select an answer that's originated from someone else's questioning and contemplate it to determine the validity of it. We don't take this answer as the gospel truth. We understand that it's dogma but don't accept or reject it. As we contemplate the answer, we cooperatively have epiphanies that may or may not be related to the original concept. Each person's sharing becomes the catalyst for others' emerging insights. Here's how the group works:

Procedure for the Insight Group

1. In a private room, individuals sit in chairs in a circle in groups of three to six people. They sit a comfortable distance apart so they can easily hear each other speaking. Each group should be a sufficient distance from other groups to lessen the possibility of distraction of members hearing others in other circles. Participants agree to share in the group for a set period of time (50 to 90 minutes).

2. The group decides on a concept to contemplate. A designated monitor (who also has the role of timer) writes this on a piece of paper and places it in the center of each circle. For example,

the concept might be, "An individual is a non-physical being, divine in nature."

3. The monitor (who can be part of a group or an outside facilitator) says, "Begin contemplating."
4. Each individual, with eyes open or closed, goes into silence and begins contemplating the concept. Each person is to regard the concept as an assumption and not an absolute truth until, in his/her own experience, he/she has come to an insight that corroborates it, expands it, or proves it not to be true.
5. When an individual feels the urge or the inner pressure to share a thought, feeling or experience, he/she should pause to let the thought, feeling, or experience develop into more clarity and then share it with the group. That which is communicated can be related or not related to the concept being contemplated. It can be in agreement or disagreement with the concept.
6. The speaker should avoid using the term "you," as this could be construed as referring to another person in the group and could run the risk of being interpreted as an evaluation. Whenever possible, the speaker should use the term "I" if the communication is really about him/herself and "we" if the communication is more theoretical. Each person should take no longer than two or three minutes to complete the communication, making sure to give others an equal amount of time to share. When the speaker is finished sharing, they place their hand on their heart to indicate their communication is complete.
7. Group members should open their eyes and silently maintain eye contact with the person speaking, without nodding, getting into a discussion, or offering agreement or disagreement or a positive or negative evaluation of any kind. The listeners should

avoid trying to facilitate the communication by asking for more details or encouraging the person to share more. Instead, they should try to understand as well as they can and accept the extent of the sharing that's been given.

8. When they've understood what's been shared, they each simply say, "Thank you" to the one who communicated.
9. If members of the group say "Thank you" before the speaker is finished, the speaker is to continue speaking until he/she has completed the thought.
10. If a member of the group doesn't completely understand what the speaker has communicated, the person can say:
    - "Say that again" to have them repeat the communication.
    - "Summarize that" if he/she hasn't understood the essence of what was said, or
    - "Clarify _______ (insert the term that wasn't understood) if he/she didn't understand a word or concept that was communicated.
11. When the communication has been completed by the speaker and understood by the listeners, all members in the group go back into silent communication, and Steps 4 through 11 are repeated when anyone else in the group chooses to share. The communication doesn't need to occur in any order. Anyone can communicate when they feel the inner necessity to do so.
12. As more communication occurs in the circle, speakers should avoid referring to anything others have said or direct their communication specifically at another as well as refrain from giving advice.
13. Five minutes before the end of the allotted time, the monitor keeping track of the time is to say, "Five more minutes;" at two

minutes remaining, the monitor says, "Two more minutes;" and, when the time period is up, the monitor says, "Complete your thought, and thank the speaker."

14. Each member of the group then takes one to two minutes to briefly share what occurred in the group that was important to them. It could be a crucial insight, a difficulty they let go of, an expansive feeling, or even just the benefit of the connection they felt with others.

THE CO-EVOLUTION TRUTH GROUP

The Truth group is similar to the Insight group except there's no central concept that everyone is contemplating. In the Truth group, the subject is self. Members sit and notice what their present-time, real experience of themselves is. Some people may find it useful to use a question such as, "What's the truth about me right now?" or "What am I experiencing in my life?" or "How am I really feeling in this present moment?" Group members endeavour to get in touch with what's going on inside without denying, minimalizing, suppressing, or dramatizing and then communicate to the group. They allow themselves to be authentic; i.e., they try to have their external self-presentation match their inner experience. "I'm feeling really shitty right now. My life sucks." Or, "I'm in a new relationship, and I'm really nervous." Or, "There's a deep inner peace that I'm getting in touch with. It feels warm and inviting."

In the safe and non-judgemental atmosphere, members can allow themselves to be nakedly honest. The sharing can be intimately human and profound. People can communicate their deepest fears, anger, sadness, or most expansive elation. They can let their emotions out. Because there are more people to relate to, the contact and acknowledgement with others is greater. They can trust, risk, and let go more easily. Often what happens in this group is a common theme appears as if by magic to which everyone connects strongly. They resonate with each other as unique viewpoints of common experience are shared and, instead of feeling alone in this co-evolutionary universe, members feel connected in this thing called life, struggling together with it and innocently trying to figure out its mystery. Especially important insights about oneself and life frequently occur. These new realization a can be immensely helpful in resolving and navigating difficult struggles.

Important Distinctions

It's important to distinguish these groups from discussion groups. In a discussion group, there's often a presentation of study material and a period of sharing where people present their ideas in a fairly linear manner as one person adds their ideas to others and agrees or disagrees as the discussion progresses. There's often a lot of interruption and communication, and understanding is frequently incomplete. Some people can get their backs up defending their position, and others can monopolize the discussion. The interchange often stays on a superficial, intellectual level, and insights aren't very deep.

In a co-evolution Insight or Truth group, there's no discussion, and the relating isn't linear. We spontaneously share without any relation to what the previous person said. Because there's no disagreement or agreement, we feel free to share whatever is really coming up sans judgment. Communication gets completed and, as a result, profound insights can occur. Even though it isn't a discussion group, the Insight or Truth groups can be a great addition to a discussion group or workshop and a wonderful way to help individuals develop deeper insights about any spiritual literature.

Here are some additional processes that can be included before either of these groups begin:

- a welcoming and introduction to the process
- a brief relaxation exercise

- a short reading of spiritual or philosophical literature (in the case of the Insight group)
- a 10- to 15-minute discussion of the central idea in the literature
- a selection of a central concept for contemplation

After the co-evolution group is finished, the following might be included:

a brief sharing of each person's important insights

a short meditation and goodbyes

"It is by going down into the abyss that we recover the treasures of life. Where you stumble, there lies your treasure. The very cave you were afraid to enter turns out to be the source of what you were looking for. The damned thing in the cave that was so dreaded has become the center."

— Joseph Campbell

COMMON INITIAL CONCERNS ABOUT THE CO-EVOLUTION GROUP AND HOW TO HANDLE THEM

These are some common concerns that first-time participants in co-evolution groups often have. It's beneficial to mention these before engaging with the group, and it's helpful after the group is finished to ask for comments on the process. These issues are frequently mentioned, and the best way to address them is by using the responses below.

Reluctance to Communicate

Initially, most first-time members find it difficult to communicate. Sometimes this is due to social shyness or the fact that they're experiencing a higher level of contact with others than they do in normal life. It should be explained that this increased attention is a benefit, and that other members' attention on a specific topic—when added to his/her own attention—augments the energy that each person has to inquire within, which makes breakthroughs in awareness much more possible. With this higher level of contact, the person may feel caught between social shyness and a deeper internal pressure to share and break through this introversion. A solution is to suggest to new members that they notice this shyness and just take the risk to communicate anyway by saying something like, "I feel shy about talking." Telling the truth about this reduces the pressure he/she may feel inside, and, in many cases, they can experience an important social breakthrough. Once this initial communication is made and the person experiences that he/she is received without judgement, it becomes easier to be a part of the group.

Lack of Feedback

Sometimes, first-time participants in a co-evolution group will state that they're uncomfortable with not being able to nod their head or say "yes" or give any other ongoing body language or verbal acknowledgement while a person is speaking. It should be explained that the purpose of refraining from these usual conversational methods is to allow the speaker to fully communicate his/her truth without any positive or negative input from the listeners. Nodding, saying "yes," or any other form of approval can subtly influence a speaker to speak more about what the listener is responding to with a nod and avoid speaking about what's really true for the speaker. It should be explained that we're socially programmed to seek acceptance from others and avoid the reality of our own experience, and we do this unconsciously when we're given subtle approval or disapproval signals from others. Participants should be told that this discomfort is temporary and will be replaced with an appreciation of how important this guideline is when they have the experience of being able to freely communicate without worrying about what others think.

Silence

Sometimes, first-time members will find the silence that occurs while members of the group contemplate to be uncomfortable. It should be explained that this is a natural experience for first-time participants because this usually doesn't occur in normal conversation. In normal conversation, people are constantly interrupted, and people are expected to come up with instant responses in a continual back-and-forth repartee. As a result, much of our relating is superficial and false, as people don't often speak the truth. It should be explained that the quality of sharing in the group isn't common in normal conversation and that this guideline has a specific purpose—we need space to look inside to contact what's real, and this requires time and silence. It's a great gift we give to others and ourselves when we do this. A suggestion could be given if this discomfort arises: to communicate to the group, "I find it difficult to be silent." This is, in fact, what's arising as a true experience for the person. Oftentimes, just this simple communication relieves the initial tension, and the person then becomes more comfortable with the silence.

Not Commenting on Another's Sharing

Some participants may find it difficult to not comment on another's communication, especially when it relates to them. It should be explained that comments on another's sharing could run the risk of being an evaluation or being interpreted as an evaluation by the previous speaker. If this happens, it can seriously affect the future sharing of a participant if he/she feels the sharing will be evaluated. It's much better to just avoid commenting than have this situation occur.

Avoiding Advice

Sometimes, people feel compelled to give advice when others present a problem. As the group's purpose isn't to solve problems, and there's no agreement for this, this should be avoided. Giving advice can also be interpreted as a subtle evaluation and, in fact, many people would prefer to solve the problem themselves. If a participant wants to give advice to another, he/she should set aside the urge until after the session and then ask the person if he/she wants advice and give it only by permission.

Wanting to Answer Another's Question

Often a person will share that they have a question or something they're confused about. For example, a person may say, "I don't know what a relationship really is." Members of the group should consider this as any other sharing, acknowledge it with a "Thank you," and avoid the temptation to give the person an answer. Participants should be allowed the dignity of struggling to find the answer for themselves, as often the answer they receive from their own contemplation is much more appropriate to their life than any answer another can give. In addition, the act of finding the answer develops the ability in that person to inquire much more deeply, so that, in the future, they'll have a greater ability to self-inspect.

The exception to this is if the person's question stimulates the same confusion in another participant. If this is so, the participant, in their own sharing, can share his/her own confusion as well as any insight they come up with in an attempt to answer the same question for themselves. However, if one has an answer to another's question and wants to help by giving the answer, this should be avoided.

The overall response to all the above concerns is that a co-evolution Insight or Truth group uses a different way of relating than in normal conversation. The guidelines in the co-evolution group have a specific purpose that's different than normal conversation: to improve the quality of the relating so that deep insight can occur. Typical, everyday conversation—even the kind of conversation that's experienced in discussion groups—can't deliver these breakthroughs in such a short period of time.

It's worth dealing with the initial discomfort of the guidelines so we can experience these insights. Once we've experienced the benefits of these new understandings, the rationale behind the guidelines will be appreciated.

Co-evolution groups can be a wonderful addition to a psychotherapy or meditation weekend or an afternoon of dyads. As people communicate and mutual understanding is established each time a communication cycle is completed, participants let go of layers of confusion, misunderstanding, and withheld pain. Relief and healing happen. Hearts open to one another. The true self shows up out of the mire of the mind and finds a new stability based on the insights of truth that each person accesses. As people collectively delve inward, the invisible cohesiveness that's inherent in life becomes self-evident, and people leave the group feeling less alone and more willing to engage in the grand scheme of awakening in their lives.

> *"The separateness seen in the world is secondary. Beyond that world of opposites is an unseen but experienced unity and identity in us all."*
>
> — Joseph Campbell

CONCLUSION

So, here we are at the end of the main body of the book.

We've come to a conclusion, but it isn't conclusive: Does the co-evolution process really work? I know it does. I'm 100% certain it does. But you'll have to decide for yourself. How? By trying out this process. Get a buddy and try out a dyad for 40 minutes, taking five-minute turns speaking and listening. Gather a few spiritual folks and do a co-evolution group. Better yet, take an Enlightenment Intensive (Coming Home Retreat). Your conclusion isn't far away.

How will you know?

When you get there.

You'll recognize your awakening when you awaken. That's the only way. And that's part of the problem on the spiritual path. You never know how close you are to an insight or awakening until it happens. Unfortunately, many of us give up just before the breakthrough. We get 95% of the way there, and then decide to go back, when all we needed to do was take one more step. The light switch is just around the corner, and we stop searching and decide to stay in the dark.

So, don't stay stuck. Don't settle for reading books about enlightenment and settling for intellectual ideas that seem to fit. Don't settle for getting temporary relief, becoming calm, or finding transitory bliss—all that fluffy New-Age stuff. Don't settle for anything less. Less is, well… just less. Actually, it's less than less. It's nothing. You're either awake or you aren't. Go for resolution. Go for transformation. Go for enlightenment. Go for the truth. Rent a guru for a little while if you need to, but don't let his dogma drive your karma. Become your own authority! Be your true source!

We folks out here in the U-n-I-verse need you. We need your unique point of view, presence, story, experience, love, understanding, all of it… all of you. I mean it...YOU. Who knows… your experience of the truth may be the next big new understanding we all need. You could be the next garage mechanic that becomes a Buddha. And the wonderful thing is, through co-evolution, you don't have to be the Lone Ranger anymore. Call it what you like—co-evolution, democratic spirituality, partner-assisted inquiry, dyadic dialoging… whatever. Don't get stuck on the label. The main thing is this: **Try it out. Be your own guru.** Come to your own conclusions. Try out this thing of you evolving me and me evolving you. No more dogma. **You have to do it by yourself, but you don't have to do it alone anymore.**

WOW!

Chapter 16

SUGGESTED CO-EVOLUTION DYADS

I've included in this book a number of my favourite dyads with the theory behind the wording and instructions on how to do them. In addition, I've also included a number of dyads under different subjects of inquiry that you can try out.

SELF-ACKNOWLEDGEMENT AND SELF-IMAGE

It's quite common for those on a path of personal unfoldment to focus excessively on aspects of themselves that need improvement, are incomplete, and need healing while ignoring the progress and accomplishments they've already made.

This tendency can draw us, over time, into a belief that we're perpetually incomplete, broken, and therefore condemned to a vicious cycle of constantly trying to fix ourselves. This is often the trap of perfectionism—the endless pursuit of never getting there… of never being satisfied with being okay in the present and believing in only future happiness. Part of this misperception results from putting our attention on what's wrong rather than seeing what's true and good about us. If we can't see the goodness in ourselves, we can't let good things happen to us in life because we feel undeserving.

An aspect of this pattern is overlooking what's true about us underneath what others consider to be undesirable. If we can't acknowledge what's true about ourselves, we'll be susceptible to the opinions of others and feel weak in our own self-image. What makes us strong in our self-image and resistant to the negative views of others is the self-recognition of what's good, honourable, and well-meaning in ourselves. Often the best way to get in touch with what's true is to contrast it with what's not true. As we get clearer on what isn't true, we become clearer about what is.

Being trapped in a negative self-image also causes us to deny the successes and achievements we've made in life, relegating us to a path of constant effort with hard-won results. We may actually have many successes, but, because we aren't recognized for and happy about them, we can feel like a failure.

In reality, success is a series of steps of small accomplishments—not just a one-time achievement. We take a small step toward a goal, complete it, and then we take another step, complete it, and soon, the larger goal is reached. For us to continue being successful, we have to enjoy the attainment of each smaller goal. If we don't let in or emotionally receive each smaller success, this can block further progress—because, in actuality, the final step in any small achievement is the enjoyment of that final step of attainment. If we don't acknowledge the completion of these intermediary steps, we may feel that each of these steps was incomplete, making the next step more difficult to take.

Part of the problem is our being socialized to not brag about ourselves. We're told we shouldn't be egotistical, or, if we fully enjoy our successes in life, disaster is just around the bend. As the stoics of our culture impute, "Happiness will be taken away if we enjoy it too much."

These dyads can help dissolve these barriers and bring about a positive self-image based on our real successes, good intentions, and genuine acts of concern for others rather than pumping ourselves up with New-Age aphorisms that someone else has created for us to repeat.

If you're new to the co-evolution process, these dyads are a great way to start. The key to the effectiveness of these dyads is to allow yourself to go ahead and brag about your accomplishments and good acts. Choose one of the A, B, C, or D self-acknowledgement dyads below, and do each for 40 minutes (five minutes each) before going onto another set.

Self-Acknowledgement Dyads

A.
Tell me something you've accomplished in life.
Thank you.
Tell me how this has helped you and others.
Thank you.

B.
Tell me something that's true about you.
Thank you.
Tell me something that isn't true.
Thank you.

C.
Hold the idea that you're okay as you are and tell me your comments.
Thank you.
Hold the idea you need to be perfect and tell me your comments.
Thank you.

D.
Tell me something you've done that was good for yourself or others.
Thank you.
Tell me something you avoided doing that was good for yourself or others.
Thank you.
Tell me any comments you have.
Thank you.

PROBLEMS

There's an old saying that there are two things in life of which you can be certain: death and taxes. There is, however, another thing of which we can be sure: having problems. We're going to have problems that irritate us, no matter what we do. They're a part of life. Everyone has them and, even though many of us tend to give the impression we've got our life together and we don't have problems, it's a guarantee that we all have them. Since this is true, it seems obvious that we should learn methods for solving them. There are certainly lots of methods that we've learned for solving problems in school—such as mathematical problems, mechanical problems, organizational problems, etc.—but we haven't been educated to solve personal problems.

This is the problem we have with problems. We often avoid them because we don't know how to solve them, thinking that avoiding them will make them go away. They don't go away—and they often get worse if we resist them. So, in this discourse, we're going to learn a few basic problem-solving methods.

Let's start by examining why problems exist.

Problems are the result of a non-understanding or a misunderstanding of something in us or between us and others, and a perceived lack of ability to engage in the activity to solve the problem For example, we may have a problem at work with completing lucrative projects that we start. We begin with a lot of excitement, and then the energy fades, and we don't understand why this happens. Other people depend on us to get things done, we don't get the project finished, they get angry at us, they think we're doing this deliberately to sabotage them, and then they stop talking to us. In this situation, something is going on inside that we and others don't understand, and we feel we don't have the ability to talk to them about it. So, we've got a big problem.

The main thing that keeps this pattern in place is a lack of understanding.

There are aspects of the problem that we don't comprehend and, as a result, they remain hidden, so we don't have sufficient information to make a decision about what to do. In addition, parts of the problem may be hooked up to other elements in the mind that they shouldn't be hooked up to. Everything is all balled up together in tight knots, one thing tied to another, and another knot entwined with something else, so we can't see all the elements separately. We may have the idea of money tied up with greed or the idea of telling the truth tied up with hurting others.

If we try to work on a solution without being fully aware of all the aspects of the problem, we can get into greater difficulty by trying to impose a solution that only works temporarily until the unknown parts of the problem resurface and drag us down again. To effectively solve a problem, we should hold off on trying to solve it right away and, instead, spend time pulling it apart, examining it, and trying to understand all aspects of it. One can call this a diagnosis or an assessment.

So, the first step is obvious: Face the problem. It won't go away if we don't face it.

The second step is to try to totally understand every aspect of the dilemma. We should communicate to another person everything about the problem so that we (and the other) can understand it completely. We shouldn't worry about being coherent or organized. We should just state it however it comes out. Let whatever emotion or upset be there as well. Let everything come out. Let ourselves discharge. Often the blocked emotions are preventing us from seeing what's really going in inside. Once this is done, we can then go to the third step: to summarize the problem as we see it in the new present moment.

Once we've taken it all apart, the third step is we reassemble it again. We put it into one- or two-sentence re-statements. We gather up everything we've said into its essence and communicate it in the dyad to the other.

The fourth step is to continue expanding and contracting the problem as in Steps 2 and 3 until we have an epiphany, such as, "Aha, this is what the problem is really all about." Often the solution is hidden in the problem, and when the essence of the problem is clear, the solution stares us in the face. With it will appear the awareness of the right actions to take. "Well, the reason I don't complete my projects is I believe that people will like me if I do a good job, but, behind the face I present to the world, I'm afraid I'm no good. I find it uncomfortable when people like me. I need to have people understand what I'm going through and just go ahead and allow myself to be liked!"

Another alternative method to solving problems is to understand their general structure—how they're put together or constructed—and then break down the problem into this structure.

If we examine any personal problem, we'll notice it has a basic, simple structure: a goal and a barrier. Any time we want something, there's something in the way of achieving it, and if we don't know how to achieve what we want, we have a problem. This is fairly obvious once we look at all problems. If we have an outcome we want to achieve, and there's nothing stopping us, we achieve it. If we have a goal and then decide we don't want it anymore, we wouldn't have a problem—e.g., "I wanted to go to university and become a brain surgeon, but I think I'd rather work at a grocery store, so I don't have a problem anymore." But, if we want something, try to get it, something stops us, and we still want it, we've got a problem.

Sometimes the problem is composed of two opposing goals. We'd like to not work so much but, to afford to not work so much, we need to make a lot of money, and that means working.

Another way we could have a problem is if there's a barrier that's impossible to remove, and the goal can't be accomplished—"I want to fly to the moon by flapping my arms." We could spend the rest of our life trying to do that and never succeed. Another problem could be that the barrier is just too big to overcome in our present state of ability. If we say we want to cut down a big old tree with a nail file, maybe we could do it in 110 years. The problem lies in the fact that we don't see the impossibility of what we want to do.

Often, dividing the problem into a goal and a barrier makes the energetic dynamic of it much clearer. Once that's clear, we can perform Steps 2, 3, and 4 above on the barrier, and then go back to restating the goal and barrier anew until the problem and its solution become clear. Choose one of the A, or B, dyads below, and do each for 40 minutes (five minutes each) before going onto another set.

Problem-Clearing Dyads

A.
Tell me everything about a problem you're having so I can understand it completely.
Thank you.
Summarize the problem as you see it now.
Thank you.
(Repeat Steps 1 and 2)

B.
Tell me a goal you have in life.
Thank you.
Tell me what's stopping you from achieving this.
Thank you.
Summarize the goal and barrier as you see it now.
Thank you.
Tell me something you can do.
Thank you.
(Repeat Steps 1, 2, 3, and 4)

ACCEPTANCE

There's a modern saying about the nature of life (attributed to John Lennon): "Life is what happens while you're busy making other plans." Oftentimes, we look back on our life at how things turned out differently than we'd planned and, in many cases, we realize things turned out better than we thought they would. In looking back at difficult circumstances, we realize these needed to occur because they made us stronger, or certain events were required to happen as a precursor to better things happening. In looking back, we see an underlying wisdom to these events. It sometimes seems there was a guiding hand or a destiny behind them even though, at the time, we resisted and couldn't accept these circumstances.

In some traditions, this so-called guiding hand would be called the Tao, or "the way of life." We might say it's the force of life or the energy of evolution.

In actuality, this energy is the nature of consciousness. It's a motivating force of growth through us as we encounter others and relate to them through challenging circumstances. Through this relating, we co-evolve and become more aware of our self, life, and others.

However, we can resist this evolution and consider it a threat. The change can undermine our basic sense of security, especially when the change is difficult and out of our comfort zone. But when this evolutionary thrust presents itself, resisting it only causes us more pain. The force of evolution builds up like rising water against a dam and, eventually, it bursts into our lives through a crisis that forces us to grow. It may be a job we hate or a relationship that isn't working for us, and we don't have the courage to take the leap out of that secure but painful situation. The force of life may jettison us out of the situation with an extreme turmoil that moves us out of our comfort zone.

One of the ways we can integrate this evolutionary change into our lives is to try to see the event from a different point of view than "this is a disaster." Once we interpret the circumstances from a different perspective and accept them as a new opportunity in our lives, we can take advantage of the new dynamic.

Acceptance Dyad

Get the idea of accepting a situation in your life that you can't accept and tell me what you experience.

Thank you.

Tell me a different point of view you could take toward this situation.

Thank you.

INNOCENCE

One of the most profound insights is discovering the essential innocence of our true nature. We've been socialized since birth to believe we're somehow flawed, imperfect, or even evil.

This programming (which I've referred to in an earlier chapter as a form of mass hypnotism) originates primarily from our Christian heritage in the West but is certainly part of other religious traditions. We've been led to believe that we're born in Original Sin and, when we're given unmonitored free will, we'll commit all kinds of harm to others and ourselves. This point of view leads us to the conclusion that we must discipline our children and each other in such a way that we remove this tendency and extract this condition of inherent badness. Generations of parents who were stuck in this point of view used all manner of punishment, shaming, and abuse to beat the perceived badness out of their children.

Taking this point of view leads us into all kinds of neurotic behaviour such as second-guessing ourselves, self-hatred, trying to be good but continually coming up short, inviting victimization as a way of self-punishment and resisting the richness of life. We're hoodwinked into thinking we need someone else or some dogmatic belief system to save us from ourselves because we can't trust looking within to follow our guidance. This creates a sense of dis-empowerment and life-long, lingering helplessness. Many groups, religious orders, and even countries have used this point of view to justify imposing their sense of goodness on others with the rationale that the end justifies their means because they think they know better and have a higher moral ground than the people they impose their will on. Many do-gooders have created more harm than good to others operating from this belief.

The solution to this is to cast this concept of Original Sin into the category of dogma, to suspend our belief in it, and then examine for ourselves the verity of whether we're inherently bad or good. This dyad will be helpful for us to explore our essential nature in the realm of innocence. It consists of contemplating innocence and its opposite so we can come up with our own conclusion. As we go back and forth in our contemplation, we'll eventually differentiate the truth from what isn't true. Choose one of the A, B or C, dyads below, and do each for 40 minutes (five minutes each) before going onto another set.

Innocence Dyads

A.
Hold the idea that you're essentially innocent and tell me what you notice.
Thank you.
Hold the idea that you're essentially sinful and tell me what you notice.
Thank you.

B.
Hold the idea that you're inherently good and tell me what you notice.
Thank you.
Hold the idea that you're inherently bad and tell me what you notice.
Thank you.

C.
Hold the idea that you grow in awareness by relating to others and tell me what you notice.
Thank you.
Hold the idea that you don't grow in awareness by relating to others and tell me what you notice.
Thank you.

THOUGHT CLARIFICATION

Often, the worst kind of problem in our relationships is the problem of knowing we have a problem but not knowing what it is. We don't quite understand why we aren't connecting to others. Sometimes it comes down to the fact that we have a thought barrier. We communicate to others with terminology and concepts that they or we don't fully understand, or we communicate to others from an understanding of concepts or terms that differs from another's understanding.

For instance, we may have a problem feeling successful because we don't understand what success actually means. When we don't understand what it is or what we're trying to accomplish, the likelihood of accomplishing it is slim. We may encounter problems in a close relationship because we may have a different understanding than our partner of what marriage is. If that's the case, we may be trying to create something that is different than what our spouse is trying to create, and we come into conflict as we try to force our definition on them.

This is far more of a problem than we realize. Frequently, the difficulties we have in any kind of relationship—at work, in our family, group, institution, or even on a broader international and political level—can be traced to something quite simple: the difference in the definitions of words. Often, we argue and can't come to an agreement because of a non-understanding or misunderstanding on a basic level in the meaning of the concepts and terminology we're using.

If we suspect that semantics may be the problem in our interactions with others, we should stop and establish a mutual understanding of some of the basic terminology we use in our discussion. A good simple question is this: "Tell me what you mean by_____," or, even simpler, "Clarify _____." Another option is to look up the word in a dictionary to see how it's commonly defined as a first step in creating an understanding.

The important point here is this—if we've determined that a disagreement in conceptual understanding has occurred, it must be corrected. We shouldn't go on with the discussion until a mutual understanding of the terminology is established. Mutual understanding means that both parties have the same definition.

In another method, called Thought Clarification, we extract what something is not from what it is. For instance, when gold undergoes a purification process, it's melted and the impurities (those substances other than gold) are removed, so the only substance left is gold. It's pure, meaning it's "nothing other than itself as itself." There's nothing other than gold mixed in with gold.

Thought Clarification works in a similar way by contemplating what a concept is in comparison to what it's not. As we differentiate anything from what it's not, we get clearer about what it actually is.

To do this, use the following exercise, which is best done in a dyad format. Here are some examples of values and concepts to start with: competency, individuality, dogma, equality, integrity, responsibility, respect, loyalty, credibility, honesty, excellence, accountability, dignity, empathy, accomplishment, courage, wisdom, compassion, friendliness, discipline, generosity, persistence, dependability.

Thought-Clarification Dyads

Tell me what ____________ is.
Thank you.
Tell me what ____________ is not.
Thank you.

Here are some suggested Thought Clarification dyads related to this book:

A.
Tell me what a spiritual path is.
Thank you.
Tell me what a spiritual path is not.
Thank you.

B.
Tell me what religion is.
Thank you.

Tell me what religion is not.
Thank you.

C.
Tell me what a guru is.
Thank you.
Tell me what a guru is not.
Thank you.

D.
Tell me what dogma is.
Thank you.
Tell me what dogma is not.
Thank you.

E.
Tell me how you can recognize dogma.
Thank you.
Tell me a decision you can make.
Thank you.

F.
Hold the idea that your life is your spiritual path, and tell me what you experience.
Thank you.
Hold the idea that your spiritual path is separate from your life, and tell me what you experience.
Thank you.

G.
Tell me what truth is.
Thank you.
Tell me what falsehood is.
Thank you.

H.
Tell me what knowledge is.
Thank you.
Tell me what knowledge is not.
Thank you.

BELIEF CLARIFICATION

In a previous chapter, we explored how we form beliefs as a result of trying to explain to ourselves the reason for an overwhelming past experience. These beliefs are often negative and self-sabotaging: "I'm no good," "Life is too hard," "Others are dangerous," and "Money is bad." As we discovered, once these beliefs are formed, they're triggered automatically and unconsciously when an experience or person similar to the overwhelming incident from the past appears in the present. We bring that unresolved charge from the past into the present, confounding and complicating the present problem, often making the current difficulty unsolvable.

Typical self-help techniques employ positive affirmations to overcome these negative beliefs, but they often don't work. People with a weak self-image originating from emotional or physical abuse may actually feel worse if they do affirmations. The positive statements only become a band-aid over the negative viewpoint and require constant repetition to be effective. The feel-good is only temporary and, when the person slides back into negativity, the failure to alter their state makes them feel worse.

These dyads operate differently than affirmations. Instead of trying to eliminate negative beliefs by replacing them with positive ones, the dyads work on rehabilitating our ability to deliberately be in opposite points of view by our own choice. In this technique, we start off choosing a belief and its opposite before the dyad begins, and then our partner inserts the wording of the belief into the instruction. We're then given the instructions to move back and forth from one belief to the other. In addition, we're asked what we did to manufacture the belief. As we continue to do this, we experience that we're actually the conscious creator of the mental and emotional state and not the unwilling victim. This can get us permanently unstuck and freed from the belief.

Belief-Clearing Dyads

Hold the idea of believing __________, and tell me what you did to get that idea.

Thank you.

Hold the idea of believing the opposite, ____________, and tell me what you did to get that idea.

Thank you.

Tell me any comments you have.

Thank you.

GUILT AND SHAME

Guilt is a common unconscious mechanism that can sabotage the best efforts of the finest souls. If you sense something is holding you back in life, you have recurring bad luck, you feel like a victim to the circumstances of life or others, and you just don't seem to get ahead in spite of your best efforts, it's likely the mechanism of guilt is involved.

To overcome the influence of guilt, it's important to understand what guilt is, how it operates, the two types of guilt (neurotic and healthy), and how to clear it.

What Guilt Is

Guilt is the feeling of remorse that arises when we make an error that hurts or adversely affects others or ourselves. It's often exacerbated by shame or self-hatred. When guilt becomes extreme, we can get stuck in a dynamic of neurotic guilt that will prevent us from enjoying the good things in life.

Neurotic Guilt

Unhealthy guilt is based on a payback mechanism that operates in this manner: When we take an action that hurts another, we mistakenly conclude that the way out of guilt is to somehow pay back our error by self-punishment. We do this by restricting our opportunity to be in a similar situation again or denying ourselves the good things in life until we feel we've paid back the debt we've created. For instance, if we've mistreated others with money—misspent it or robbed others—we think the solution is to prevent ourselves from having more money or allowing it to slip from our grasp as a way of preventing further hurt. The underlying error is that we don't trust ourselves to treat others well regarding money.

The problem with this solution is that the payback action is usually far more severe and lasts longer than the original transgression. In addition, we add self-shaming into the mix, diminishing our self-worth by negative conclusions such as, "I'm no good," "I'm bad," or "I'm worthless," mistakenly thinking we'll pay up the debt by putting ourselves down. This is a false solution that creates more problems. As we get stuck in the attitude of "I'm bad," the only behaviours that emerge from this state are self-destructive. The ensuing actions only reinforce the self-conclusion of "I'm bad," which imprisons us in a vicious cycle of self-shaming, self-deprecation, bad actions, and being right about being wrong.

The Way Out of Guilt

The first thing to understand about guilt is that shaming our self is illogical. In our basic nature, we're good. Indeed, it's only because we're good in our hearts that we feel guilty about the bad things we've done. If we were inherently bad, we wouldn't feel bad about the bad things we've done. We'd feel indifferent. We wouldn't care.

In reality, we feel bad because we're good at heart. This is self-evident in the way we feel when we do something we consider to be bad. Therefore, to shame ourselves is inconsistent with our true nature.

Fortunately, there's a healthy way out of guilt. The way is to become conscious of our mistakes, learn from them, and contact our inner standard to guide us to make better choices in similar situations in the future. As we do this, we develop the confidence and trust that we'll behave more ethically and honestly. We then know we'll be less likely to make the same mistakes again, and we can allow good things into our lives.

The Process of Guilt Clearing

There's a process involving dyad work that, if followed, can significantly relieve us of unhealthy guilt and naturally bring good things into life.

1. Understand the Two Categories of Guilt

There are errors of commission and errors of omission—i.e., actions we did and actions we didn't do about which we feel bad. When referring to guilt, we often assume this is related only to actions we committed. But guilt can also be related to actions we could have taken but didn't; i.e., the failure to do something. For example: "I saw the person drowning, and I could have jumped into the water and rescued her, but I didn't."

2. Acknowledge

One of the most powerful things we can do in the process of releasing guilt is to simply acknowledge the naked fact of our mistake—to just state it with no embellishment—for example, saying "I yelled and screamed at my innocent child," without any justification or storytelling.

Often, we're able to sidestep the impact of our transgression by attempting to justify our action. "He'd been ripping people off in his business for years, so I was just giving him a taste of his own medicine by robbing him." We can try to dilute the impact of our actions by telling a long story about it: "Well, it all started way back in '89 when she looked at me in an odd way, and I kind of wondered what she was thinking. Then in '91, she..." All of this just dilutes our feeling of guilt. We must look at the main event—the simple fact of what we did or didn't do.

Even more powerful is creating a dyad in which we can confess to another person what we did. It's important that the listening person simply hear what we have to say without judging or giving advice on what to do. When we're done, the person acknowledges with a simple, "Thank you." There's a great release in just telling the truth. We can also confess it to God, a Higher Power, the Great Spirit, the universe, or whatever represents to us some higher form of wisdom. What's important is to get this communication from the inside to the outside for a release to occur.

It's also important to say what we did or didn't do in our own estimation. When we use someone else's standard—for example, that of the law or the church—it can be a subtle way of avoiding taking responsibility. "It really wasn't that bad because I don't agree with what the church dictates." It needs to be an error that we judge to be hurtful in our estimation according to what's in our own heart. By doing this, we're developing our own standards of conduct and bringing our hearts into alignment with our mind.

3. Feel Guilty

This appears to be counter-instructive to what was just said above about feeling bad. Even though we're good in our nature, we should allow ourselves to feel bad about our transgressions but without the shaming. Why? Because, when we allow ourselves to feel bad, we break through the barrier of denial: "I hit him because he looked like he was judging me, and yes, he was bloody, but it didn't really hurt him that much." On the other side of this barrier is the stark truth of the transgression that was made. It's the acknowledgement of the full truth of our errors and the feeling of the remorse that motivates us to learn from our mistakes and change our behaviour.

4. Retro-inspect

We should then look at what we could have done or not done differently. There's an old saying that hindsight is 20/20. In looking back at our errors and the effects of our actions on others and ourselves, we can distinguish more clearly what was right from what was wrong. In retrospection, we learn from our mistakes and discover that, in our hearts, we really want to treat others well. This will give us confidence that we can make the right future decisions in similar situations. Knowing that we can create a different positive outcome allows us to let in good things in the future.

5. Learn

We should ask, "What have I learned from this?" Developing wisdom from our transgressions gives us even more confidence that we can make the right decisions in the future. In the past, we denied ourselves good things because we didn't trust ourselves to make the right decisions about money, sex, power, love, etc. But the real problem was less about trusting ourselves and more about learning from our mistakes. When we know better, we'll let our lives get better. We'll trust ourselves to not abuse the good things in life and, therefore, allow more abundance in money, relationships, opportunities, etc. to flourish. We must remedy this. The question, "What have I learned from this?" also brings us into alignment with the purpose of life. If the true purpose of life is the development of consciousness, by inspecting what we've learned from our actions/inactions and acquiring self-knowledge from our mistakes, we move more into the natural flow of life.

6. Establish a Standard

The final step is to establish our standards. By learning from our mistakes, we also access intuitive ethical and moral guidelines that we can self-reference in any situation in the future: "I learned that other people have the same feelings as me, and they get hurt in just the same way." There's an inner criterion here, a standard of treating others and bringing it to awareness. When we do this, it strengthens our moral character. We become more confident that we'll act for the benefit of ourselves and others and allow goodness into our lives. It turns out that our inner standard is very similar to the golden rule: "Treat others as you would have them treat you." But it's much deeper than this. It's connected to our true nature. We should treat others better because, in our true nature, we actually *are* others. When we mistreat others, we're actually causing harm to the whole fabric of our common, unified existence. We harm our co-evolution together. On the other hand, because almost any progress in life is somehow associated with how we treat others, when we treat others better, we become more successful.

In summary, by practicing these steps, we can release our neurotic self-punishment, gain discrimination for future actions, and move into greater harmony with the inherent co-evolutionary dynamic in life.

Here's an example of the steps of guilt-clearing:

"I took money from my boss by entering phony petty cash bills into his books and taking the money. What I'd do differently is talk to him about my financial difficulties and either ask for a raise or an advance. I learned that, when I'm desperate for money, I should be honest and tell the truth first."

Guilt-Clearing Dyads

We begin working through these instructions within the five-minute period. Any instructions that we don't get through we should work on in the next five-minute period before beginning again on the first instruction. Choose one of the A or B dyads below, and do each for 40 minutes (five minutes each) before going onto another set.

A.

Tell me something you did that you think you shouldn't have done in your own estimation.

Thank you.

Tell me what you'd do differently, if you could, looking back on this.

Thank you.

Tell me what you learned from this.

Thank you.

Tell me something you failed to do that you think you should have done in your own estimation.
Thank you.
Tell me what you'd do differently, if you could, looking back on this.
Thank you.
Tell me what you learned from this.
Thank you.

B.
Tell me a standard you have for treating others better.
Thank you.
Tell me a standard you have for treating yourself better.
Thank you.

CRITICALNESS

There's a mechanism of the mind that causes suffering in working or family relationships. It's a mental activity that we secretly hide from others as a black secret. Fortunately, this tendency, when rightly understood and properly dealt with, can bring about mutual understanding, better relationships, and connection to others.

This mechanism is called criticalness. We all have a sense of it. It's that automatic irritation we feel about others' behaviour. It's the silent mental put-down in which we typify another as beneath us and less than human. It's that labeling of an individual as a jerk, idiot, phony, egotist, sexist, prude, nit-picker, airhead, etc. (you can add your own favourite names to the list). It's the compulsion within us to condemn and judge others.

In the play, *No Exit* by Jean Paul Sartre, a character complains, "Hell is other people." Deeply critical people take this point of view to the extent that they secretly dwell in a hell of condemnation, in which others, not themselves, are the main problem in life. As they gradually push well-meaning people away, their lot in life becomes a state of loneliness and misery.

Being around individuals who condemn us can be difficult. We feel we can't fully be ourselves and must constantly watch our actions. We hold back our true thoughts, suppress our feelings and resort to acting the way they want us to behave. But, as we do this, unreality and emotional coldness enter the relationship, and we find ourselves pulling away and establishing distance from them. We're compelled to do this as a natural, protective mechanism when we'd really like to be open to them.

Unfortunately, modern television, through the proliferation of half-hour sitcoms, has elevated criticalness to the level of an art-form with the use of the one-liner put-down or the snide remark that generates canned laughter with an off-the-cuff, underhanded insult.

However, if we engage in this type of comic relating in our relationships, life becomes a tragedy. Criticalness can contribute to people lashing out and emotionally injuring others over the most insignificant incidents. After the deed has been done, there's no laughter. People wonder what happened and feel deeply guilty about their behaviour. The parasitic legacy of criticalness is that it can kill any relationship, whether at work or at home.

Fortunately, there are steps to take to deal with criticalness in ourselves and others. I'd like to introduce these to you now.

1. Acknowledge

The first step is to acknowledge the lack of value that criticalness has in your life. Ask yourself if you've honestly felt any better after entertaining negative judgements of others. Try this exercise:

Think a condemning thought of another person.

Notice how you feel.

Think a loving thought of another person.

Notice how you feel.

Then ask yourself: "Does criticalness make me feel any better? Has it honestly improved my life?"

Now ask yourself: "What's it like to be on the receiving end of another's belittlement? Does it uplift me?"

If you're truthful, you'll admit that criticalness hasn't made you any happier in life. In fact, I've never met a person who, after looking into their heart, said they felt good about a workday thinking critical thoughts of others or expressing criticism during coffee breaks and lunch. The first step is to acknowledge that condemnation of others hasn't enriched your life.

2. Choose

The second step is a natural outcome of the first: Decide to dissolve your criticalness. Choose to do something about it. Right here and now, make it a project to overcome criticalness in yourself. It may be true that you've been hurt by others' belittlement and you'd like to deal with that first. But, if you're going to be successful in this effort, concentrate at the beginning on handling your own criticalness. The more you understand where your judgements come from, the more you'll understand the origin of them in others. In this way, you'll be less affected by others' criticalness. In addition, the less you're irritated by others, the more likely others will treat you well.

3. Understand the Origin

The third step to dissolving criticalness is to understand the origin of criticalness. If the source of our criticalness isn't within others, where does it come from? One person aptly answered this question when they observed, "When you point your finger at another person, you've got three other fingers pointing back at yourself!" It's in us.

Carl Jung, the psychologist, has given some illumination on this. He discovered a mechanism in the mind that he called projection, whereby the individual takes aspects of his shadow side (the perceived negative, unintegrated side of one's unconsciousness) and projects or perceives this in others. Criticalness is related to this mechanism.

The reason we become judgemental of others is because we see in them the things we don't want to acknowledge in ourselves. We project onto others the characteristics of ourselves that we have a hard time facing in our lives. So, if I'm critical of Harry for being a jerk, it's because, in some way, I've done something that's similar to what he's doing, and I'm feeling uneasy about it. Others are mirroring us without even trying to.

The second reason we become critical is related to misunderstanding. When something isn't understood between two individuals, criticalness can arise. It occurs when, in your estimation, you think there's something that another person hasn't understood about you that you want them to understand but that you haven't fully communicated to them. Saying this in a different way, if I sense that another person hasn't received a communication about myself that I feel is important for him to understand, I become critical. However, I'm responsible for this because I haven't gotten myself across to him. There may have been a number of reasons why he didn't understand: he didn't hear me, he was preoccupied, he was distracted, he interrupted me, or he just didn't want to hear me. Whatever the reason, I didn't get across something about myself that I thought was important, and I want him to understand what this is. It's up to me to get the person to listen and understand me.

It's also important to distinguish between being upset and criticalness. Criticalness is a mental state of finding fault in another and dwelling on it. Upset is different. Someone may not show up for an appointment after making a commitment to do so, and I may get upset, but I might not judge them for this. However, criticalness can often get enmeshed with upset and add more anger to the upset if I judge someone negatively.

4. Just Stop It

The fourth step in removing criticalness is: Stop expressing it. That's right. Just notice when you're finding fault in others and stop verbalizing it. Now, this may seem like suppression, and, in a way, it is, but you'll feel better for it. Because underneath our justification of our fault finding, we know we're participating in telling a lie. We know, in our hearts, we're doing the best we can in life, and we know the same is true for others. It's untrue that others are bad. In verbalizing our criticalness, we're also injuring others. Even though the person we judge isn't there, we know we're poisoning another's point of view toward the person we're going on about. We feel guilty about this and, as a way of compensating for our bad act, we keep good things out of our life.

5. Self-inspection

The fifth step in removing criticalness is to practice self-inspection. Whenever you notice yourself finding fault in others, ask yourself, "What is it I'm being critical of in others? How am I similar to them?"

The key word here is "similar." You may be critical of others because they lack control of their food consumption, and what's similar in you is a lack of control in planning your business activities. Sometimes, it takes a while, but, when you hit the similarity, an amazing thing happens: your criticalness dissolves into nothingness. You become open to that person again, and you've established a commonality with them ("Wow, they're working on the same thing I'm working on!"). You begin to have more compassion for them. In addition, you begin to be easier on yourself for your own faults as you notice that you're not alone in your imperfections. Sometimes, as a side effect, you'll begin to seek to improve your own behaviour. Finally, you'll naturally tend to treat others better out of real understanding of human nature.

Another thing you can do is ask yourself this question, "What is it that I feel is important about myself that I think another doesn't understand?" When you're clear about this, communicate this to the other person so you're talking about yourself without laying a trip on them.

For example, there's a difference between these two communications:

"You make me angry every time you leave the toilet seat up, you idiot!" AND

"What you should know about me is that I like to keep the toilet seat down."

The first statement is a put-down of the other person and makes them responsible for your upset. The second statement is a simple communication about yourself that will lessen the tendency for others to get defensive and resist you. When your communication is complete, you'll notice a remarkable dissolution in your criticalness and greater openness to the person in question.

Also, avoid participating in criticalness with others or change the subject or just ignore it.

The problem of criticalness can gradually dissolve if it's taken on as a long-term project. These techniques are self-reinforcing, which means that simply by experiencing the moments when your fault-finding dissolves and you feel freed from being critical, you'll tend to make these techniques automatic. Choose one of the A or B dyads below, and do each for 40 minutes (five minutes each) before going onto another set.

Criticalness-Dissolution Dyads:

A.

Tell me what you're critical of in another.
Thank you.
Tell me something you've done or a way you're similar to this.
Thank you.

B.

Tell me what's important about yourself that you think another doesn't understand.
Thank you.
Tell me what you can do to bring about this understanding.
Thank you.

LOVE

Love is one of the most beautiful emotions in the universe. Without love, life would feel flat and one-dimensional. We wouldn't experience a connection to each another. Children wouldn't be nurtured and be able to grow mentally and emotionally. We wouldn't feel safe enough to expose our vulnerabilities to one another and release our pain and suffering. It's the glue that holds the universe together. It's the infinite, timeless catalyst that draws us all together so we can relate and evolve.

The following dyads help us get in touch with love, expose the blocks we have to its experience, and get out of our mind and into our heart. Each section should be a 40-minute period.

Love Dyads

A.
Tell me what love is.
Thank you.

B.
Be open to the presence of love and tell me what you experience.
Thank you.

C.
Tell me how you want to be loved.
Thank you.
Tell me how you want to love others.
Thank you.

D.
Tell me a way that you've withheld love from others that wasn't the best in your estimation.
Thank you.
Tell me what you've learned from this.
Thank you.

ENLIGHTENMENT

The following questions are commonly used in Enlightenment Intensives or Coming Home Retreats. There's a difference between these questions and the insight questions. With these questions, we're attempting to arrive at a direct experience of our object of inquiry, not a new intellectual comprehension. To understand the difference between an insight and direct experience, you can review Chapter 6, Personal Reality and Ultimate Truth, where this is discussed.

Our goal with these questions is to go beyond mental constructs, beliefs, and concepts to an experience of the essential nature of life, self, others, love, etc. With these questions, the listener's guidelines are the same, but you start off with a slightly different approach in your investigation. When you get the instruction from your partner, you need to start off with a real sense of the subject you're investigating to make sure you aren't just dabbling around in theoretical musing. After receiving the instruction, start by selecting a real experience of your object (life, self, another, love, etc.) that's occurring right in the moment. If you're inquiring into the nature of yourself, what's most real might be the pumping of your heart, the sensation of breathing, or the discomfort of back pain. If it's life, choose a piece of life like a tree, a flower, or a sensation in your body that's palpably real in the moment. It's the same with the other questions. Then, hold that experience in your consciousness and place your attention on that object with the intention that you directly experience the essence of it. In the case of self, you want to become directly conscious of the one who's having the sensation of the heart beating or breathing or back pain. In the other questions, your goal is the same: to experience the true nature of life, another, love, etc. within that object. We then proceed to the next steps of being open and communicating to your partner. One question should be worked on for the 40-minute period.

For the serious seekers of truth, these questions are very compelling, drawing us into the deep mystery of existence and nourishing the deep yearning we've felt for the truth. One, 40-minute period of dyading on one of these questions isn't enough, but it can give you a taste of the power of the co-evolution process on these subjects. If you're seriously interested in awakening, you should enroll in an Enlightenment Intensive or Coming Home Retreat, where you'll be supported in moving through the stages of awakening that were described earlier in Chapter 13, The Enlightenment Intensive.

Four Fundamental Enlightenment Dyads

A.
Tell me who you are.
Thank you.

B.
Tell me what you are.
Thank you.

C.
Tell me what another is.
Thank you.

D.
Tell me what life is.
Thank you.

Alternative Dyads

A.
Tell me what love is.
Thank you.

B.
Tell me what consciousness is.
Thank you

ENLIFENMENT

It's common after an awakening in any tradition for the openness to the new consciousness to last anywhere from two weeks to a few months before the expansiveness of the experience fades. You may still retain the knowingness of the truth, but you can become disconnected from perceiving yourself or life from the new awareness. You know what you know, and you know you know, but you may not be experiencing what you know. Someone who's been to a mountaintop and has seen the valley and the panoramic vista may still be in the exalted experience when they return to the valley, but the feeling eventually subsides. What remains is the knowledge of the difference between being at the peak and living in the valley.

The fading of direct experience is a result of the undissolved parts of the ego or mind gradually reforming around the self and the lack of cultivation of the awakening experience. Let me explain this further.

You may have a direct experience or have realized a divine truth of yourself, but there's still more knowledge to gain from that experience. You fall in love with someone, but that's not the end of the relationship. It takes the rest of your life to get to know that person. There are barriers that come up in your relationship that need to be dissolved as you get closer to each other. It's the same with enlightenment. You've finally come home to yourself. You're in a new relationship with yourself. This is actually the beginning of the spiritual path, not the end! It's the start of a new life of being in truth when most of your self has been in illusion. I have called this process enlifenment, and it's enhanced with four processes: Clearing, attention, knowledge, and self-remembrance.

Clearing

With enlightenment, you've dislodged the foundation of your mind. Before enlightenment, the basis of the mind was illusion, and now it's truth. Many of your dysfunctional ways of being, false solutions to life, traumas, and limiting beliefs are still hanging around. They've metaphorically hit the fan, and they're scattered all over the wall. They're still alive and kicking and will try to re-establish their sovereignty. When they do, you start to feel unbalanced and disoriented. You start to wonder, "What the hell's going on? I thought I got enlightened. How come I'm feeling so unenlightened?" What's happened is that you've turned the light on in yourself, so to speak, with your enlightenment experience. You're becoming aware of the conflicts within yourself that have always been there. Now you see and feel them. You're conscious of them.

You can run away from them, hide from them by adopting a phony spiritual personality, or face them. There's now an opportunity to dissolve these so you can be more fully in the radiance of your truth. Many of the solitary meditation spiritual practices (that may have gotten you enlightened) are a slow way to dissolve them. It's faster to engage in some short-term psychotherapy or energy work. The best forms are methods that are insight oriented; i.e., processes that, with the help of a skilled practitioner, bring you to your own understanding of how you've constructed your mind and ego and then assist you to dissolve them.

Attention

If, after your awakening, you go right back into regular life and focus exclusively on the externals of existence—all the activities of your job, parental duties, watching TV, etc.— the lack of attention to the awakening experience can cause it to fade. If you haven't developed some strategy for how to live from this new awareness—particularly as you're relating to others—you can default into old patterns of relating and lose touch with the spiritual experience.

What you need to do is use your new awareness of yourself as your object of concentration in meditation. Instead of using your breath, a mantra, a picture, body sensation, etc. as your focus, use the truth of what you know as your focus: "I'm just myself," "I'm love," "I'm everything." Start your day connected to this awareness, and come home to it at night. The more you place your attention on the truth of your being, the more you'll being in yourself with your "doing-ness" in the world.

Knowledge

You've directly experienced the truth, but there's still more to know. Maybe you've experienced that you're the ONE. You're the whole thing in the universe. You are IT! It's a big deal that's not such a big deal. It's a huge realization, but, at the same time, it's just the fact of existence. It's just the way things are, so what's the big deal? You shouldn't stop there. There's more to know about you. For instance, what are the characteristics of yourself? What are you composed of? What are your qualities—consciousness, love, infinite potential, happiness? Get the idea? There's a huge list. So, put your attention on yourself, and then investigate the immense fullness that's within. The more you become aware of and differentiate all the different aspects of your true self, the more these come into balance. You'll be more able to access these divine qualities in yourself and engage them in your relationships with others. When you're aware that pure consciousness or divine love is part of your true nature, the you'll be better able to relate to others with a clear mind and pure heart.

Self-remembrance

Many people on the path of consciousness feel there's a separation between the spiritual and everyday life when, in fact, there isn't. This separation is self-created. Everyday life is the testing and stabilizing ground for the spiritual experience if the former two practices are used. The practice of self-remembering is essential to bridging this gap. It's an extension of the attention exercise. Whenever you're around or in a conversation with others, put your attention on yourself. Begin when you're a listener. Be in the space of your essential nature and keep your attention on yourself as you interact. Let the genuineness and open-heartedness flow from there. This, of course, will challenge you to stay centered in yourself. You'll fall in and out of your connection as you begin this practice, but, with more interaction with others, you'll develop your ability to stay in touch with yourself. In this way, you begin to realize that life isn't antagonistic to being who you really are. It's actually the optimal school for training you to "be you to fullness" in your everyday relating to others.

With these ideas in mind, the following are some dyads designed for the purpose of helping you be more connected to your enlightenment as you navigate in the world. Choose one of the A, B, C D or E dyads below, and do each for 40 minutes (five minutes each) before going onto another set.

Enlifenment Dyads

A.
Put your attention on a direct experience you've had and tell me what you notice.
Thank you.

B.
Tell me a difficulty you have presenting your true self to others.
Thank you.
Tell me a decision you could make to live more from your true self.
Thank you.

C.
Tell me a challenge you have with living from an awakening experience you've had.
Thank you.
Tell me what you can do in your life to cultivate living more from this state.
Thank you.

D.
Tell me what enlightenment is.
Thank you.
Tell me what enlightenment is not.
Thank you.

E.
Put your attention on your true self and tell me a quality you notice.

Thank you.
Let this quality expand in your awareness and tell me what you experience.
Thank you.

Other dyads that are valuable would be the ones on Authenticity.

CREATING YOUR OWN INSTRUCTION

There are obviously more aspects of self, life, and others into which we can inquire that aren't covered in this book. I leave it up to you to create your own areas of inquiry based on your interest. Sometimes, it can be a challenge to put a subject of investigation into an instruction, so here are some guidelines. One way to do this is to discuss with your dyad partner an issue that has your attention in life and brainstorm with her/him on an appropriate wording. In general, we should try to put the instruction into the "Tell me" form, with the "Tell me" at the beginning of the sentence and the verb near the end.

Sometimes you may be faced with an issue that you can't fully articulate, so a good question to start off with is: "Tell me something you're confused about," or "Tell me what you have a hard time describing."

Once you've given a response to the question, have your partner put the subject into the form of: "Tell me everything about ___________ (inserting the subject) so I can understand it completely." Or, "Tell me what it is about yourself in regard to ___________ (inserting the subject) that you think others don't understand."

For example, you might say, "I have a hard time describing my feelings about a man I just met." You'd then get your partner to give you the instruction: "Tell me everything about your feelings about the man you just met so I can understand them completely."

It may become apparent that you can use an instruction in a different section such as in the Belief-Clearing section.

Some of the most powerful work can come out of being faced with an issue you want to avoid. Here are some questions you can have your partner ask you to get at these issues and begin to resolve them.

Dyads

A.
Tell me an issue that you find difficult to talk about.
Thank you.

B.
Tell me a question that you don't want others to ask you.
Thank you.

C.
Tell me something you find hard to face in yourself.
Thank you.

For example, you might say in response to A, B, or C, "Something I find hard to face in myself is my inability to deal with conflict in my relationship." You'd then get your partner to give you the instruction:

"Tell me everything about your inability to deal with conflict in your relationship so I can understand it completely."

Sometimes, a "why" inquiry may come up in response to A, B, or C. For example, in response to B, you might say: "A question I don't want others to ask me is, 'Why do I let others take advantage of me.'" Avoid getting your partner to ask a "why" question, as this type of question can illicit an intellectual response or move a person into justifying or rationalizing their behaviour rather than understanding what's underneath the behaviour that's causing it. A much better format is to word the instruction in terms of a barrier: "Tell me what stops you from asserting yourself around others," or "Tell me what it is in yourself that allows others to take advantage of you."

Creating your own instructions is a bit of an art, but once you've done a number of the different dyads in this book, you'll be able to do this. You may find that just varying the wording slightly can make a big difference in the effectiveness of the instruction penetrating right to the core of the issue. Experiment with this and have fun with it.

ADDITIONAL CO-EVOLUTION DYADS

Work on one section (the sections are divided by spaces) for the full time of the dyad (40 minutes)

Being Yourself

Tell me some concerns you have about being yourself around others.

Thank you.

Tell me a decision you could make.

Thank you.

Decide to be happy with yourself right now and tell me what you experience.

Thank you.

Understanding

Tell me something about yourself that you think others don't understand.

Thank you.

Tell me a decision you could make.

Thank you.

Confusion

Tell me something in regard to ________ (insert topic) that you aren't clear about.

Thank you.

Tell me something in regard to ________ (insert topic) that you are clear about.

Thank you.

Goals

Tell me a goal you have in your life.

Thank you.

Tell me how you can be responsible to make this happen.

Thank you.

Tell me something you think God wants for you.

Thank you.

Tell me something you want for yourself.

Thank you.

Success and the Law of Attraction

Tell me something you want to achieve in life.

Thank you.

Tell me a goal you believe you can achieve.

Thank you.

Feel really good about achieving this and tell me what you experience.

Thank you.

Completion

Tell me something you haven't yet completed in your life.

Thank you.

Tell me a decision you could make.

Thank you.

Personal Values

Tell me what ____________is.

Thank you.

Tell me what ____________is not.

Thank you

Examples: competency, individuality, equality, integrity, responsibility, respect, loyalty, credibility, honesty, excellence, accountability, dignity, empathy, accomplishment, courage, wisdom, compassion, friendliness, discipline, generosity, persistence, dependability.

Self and Other (both partners work on the same questions)

Tell me what you are.

Thank you.

Tell me what another is.

Thank you.

Authenticity

Tell me the truth about the way it is for you right now.

Thank you.

Be here and now in your real self and tell me what you notice.

Thank you.

Tell me something about yourself that you think others don't understand.

Thank you.

Tell me something you can do to be understood.

Thank you.

Decide to be in your life fully and tell me what you notice.

Thank you.

Decide to not be in your life fully and tell me what you notice.

Thank you.

Body Awareness

Put your attention on your body and tell me what you notice.

Thank you.

Tell me everything about a physical challenge you're having and how it feels in your body.

Thank you.

If this physical challenge could speak, tell me what it would say.

Thank you.

Co-dependency

Tell me a way you've depended on others for your happiness.

Thank you.

Tell me another way you can find happiness.

Thank you.

Tell me how you've depended on others to complete you.

Thank you.

Tell me a decision you could make.

Thank you.

Tell me how you've put yourself second in relationships with others.

Thank you.

Tell me a decision you could make.

Thank you.

Tell me what you do to get others to like you.

Thank you.

Tell me a decision you could make.
Thank you.

Tell me about you not trusting your own feelings.
Thank you.
Tell me what you can do to trust your own feelings.
Thank you.

Tell me how you've compared yourself to others.
Thank you.
Tell me a decision you could make.
Thank you.

Boundaries

Tell me a way you'd like others to relate to you.
Thank you.
Tell me a way you'd like to relate to others.
Thank you.

Communication

Tell me some concerns you have about listening honestly to others.
Thank you.
Tell me some concerns you have about speaking honestly to others.
Thank you.

Tell me a way you deny telling the truth to others.
Thank you.
Tell me what you find difficult to face.
Thank you.
Tell me how you can develop the ability to tell the truth to others.
Thank you.

Personal Power

Tell me how you give away your personal power to others.

Thank you.

Tell me what you're reluctant to face in yourself and present to others.

Thank you.

Rejection

Tell me a way you've felt rejected or criticized by another.

Thank you.

Tell me a way you've rejected or criticized others.

Thank you.

Tell me a way you've felt rejected or criticized by another.

Thank you.

Tell me how you've rejected or criticized yourself.

Thank you.

Tell me what you can do to handle your feelings of rejection or criticalness in the future.

Thank you.

Intimacy

Tell me something you've done in a relationship that helped you get closer to another.

Thank you.

Tell me something you've done in a relationship that wasn't helpful in getting closer to another.

Thank you.

Imagine yourself getting close to another and tell me what you experience.

Thank you.

Tell me a decision you can make to get closer to others.

Thank you.

Help

Tell me how you can help your partner in your relationship get closer to you.

Thank you.

Tell me how your partner can help you.

Thank you.

For Couples

Tell me something you like about me.

Thank you.

Tell me something you think we agree on.

Thank you.

Tell me something about yourself you think I should know.

Thank you.

Tell me an error you've made in our relationship.

Thank you.

Tell me what you've learned from this error.

Thank you.

Tell me something you'd do differently in a similar situation in the future.

Thank you.

Tell me something you're grateful for in our relationship.

Thank you.

Tell me something you want to thank me for.

Thank you.

Responsibility

Tell me something you blame another for.

Thank you.

Tell me something that person is responsible for.

Thank you.

Tell me what you're responsible for.

Thank you.

Personality

Be in the personality of ______________ and tell me about yourself.

Thank you.

Tell me what you're trying to do by being in the personality of ______________.

Thank you.

Tell me a decision you could make.

Thank you.

(Examples of personalities: controller, self-critic, procrastinator, protector, victim, saboteur, hero, lost child, caretaker, scapegoat, mascot, hippie, late arriver, saint, saviour, rebel, vixen, goddess, enabler, rescuer, clown, perfectionist, etc.)

Self-Empowerment

Be in the personality of ______________ and tell me what you notice.

Thank you.

Feel good about being ______________ and tell me what you experience.

(Examples: creator, leader, teacher, adventurer, pioneer, asserter, decider, prosperous one, peacemaker, healer, communicator, risk-taker, etc.)

Money

Tell me what money is.

Thank you.

Tell me what money is not.

Thank you.

Give me an example of how money is good.

Thank you.

Give me an example of how money is bad.

Thank you.

Tell me any comments you have about money.

Thank you.

Tell me how you want to earn money in a way that uplifts yourself and others.

Thank you.

Tell me how you want to spend money in a way that uplifts yourself and others.

Thank you.

Compulsions/Addictions

Tell me a behaviour of yours that's compulsive or addictive in your own estimation.

Thank you.

Tell me in detail what you normally do when you engage in this behaviour.

Thank you.

Tell me a behaviour of yours that's compulsive or addictive in your own estimation.

Thank you.

Hold the idea of having the urge to engage in this behaviour and not doing it, and tell me what you experience.

Thank you.

Tell me what you can do to get support to face this behaviour.

Thank you.

These are just few of the many dyads that you can do. For a free 4 page list of these dyads please e-mail; support@awakentheguruinyou.com.

To download a free 5 minute dyad timing gong go to: www.awakentheguruinyou.com and click on "store" and "CD's

THE STORY OF YOUR HEART

Tell me the story of your heart
It is much different than the other stories you have told
And deeper…
Its springs from the hills
Off in the forest
And flows to the valley
Through the coltsfoot, the fern and the wild ginger root
Through the bubbling pool
Where the whitetail deer quench their thirst,
To the deep pond
Where the brooke trout dart
And the cattails congregate
To hear the bullfrogs burp their blathering conversation.

I will sit by the edge
Gazing at the still cool water reflecting your face
And the brilliant evening stars
And revel… in the grandeur
Of who you really are.
Russell Scott May 2005

RESOURCES

For information on Russell's Coming Home Retreats (Enlightenment Intensives), other retreats, and mentorship sessions go to: www.awakentheguruinyou.com

or e-mail Russell at: support@awakentheguruinyou.com

His Facebook page: https://www.facebook.com/awakentheguruinyou/

Check out Russell's music at: www.russellscottfolk.com

SOME FREE STUFF ON RUSSELL'S WEBSITE

"Living from the Inside Out": a 25-page guide on the five paths of awakened living.

Many free articles including:

Why I Don't Recommend a Sub-Arachnoid Hemorrhage to Get Enlightened"

"How to Get a License to Be Yourself"

"The Wisdom of the Gasping Man"

Ask for a **free download of a five-minute gong timer** CD so you can start doing dyads with your circle of friends.

There have been a few books written about or that reference the Enlightenment Intensive or Coming Home Retreat. These are some good ones that I recommend:

The Enlightenment Intensive: The Power of Dyad Communication for Self-Realisation by Lawrence Noyes. Zen Ways Press.

Tell Me Who You Are, by Jake Chapman. Contact: Jake and Eva Chapman, The Old Manor House, The Green, Hanslope, MKI9 7LS (free download at: http://www.enlightenment-intensives.org.uk/TellMeWhoYouAre%28part1%29.pdf)

The Quantum Gods: The Origin and Nature of Matter and Consciousness, by Jeff Love. Available from iUniverse.com, Barnes and Noble, Amazon.com (contains info on the Enlightenment Intensive).

ENLIGHTENMENT INTENSIVES AROUND THE WORLD

To find facilitators of the Enlightenment Intensive in your area, Google: "Enlightenment Intensive."

https://www.enlightenment-intensive.net/

https://www.sandoth.com/

There are many people that give Enlightenment Intensives around the world. Sometimes they give the retreat under different names: Illumination Intensive, True Awakening, True Heart/True Mind, etc. Some give a traditional intensive according to the original version originated by Charles Berner, and some have altered it. If you're interested in doing one of my retreats, a retreat facilitated by people who've studied with me, or to be referred to a facilitator I recommend, contact me at: russell@awakentheguruinyou.com

WITH GRATITUDE

There are a number of people to whom I want to express my gratitude. They've all, in various ways, contributed to the life of this book:

Ellen Forrester, my partner, for her enthusiastic spirit and sustaining love. Darlene Nicholson, Lise Gillis, Victor Levytsky, Reinier de Smit, Sandy Fiegehen, Merryl Chopra, and Brenda McMorrow, who've provided such wonderful support as ongoing staff and friends on my retreats; my three children, Jesse, Jonathan, and Leela, who've kept me honest and authentic; Heather Embree, Sandy Fiegehen and Lynn Gray for their editing and support of me personally and professionally; my previous wife, Linda, who was my companion through thick and thin as we explored this path of co-evolution for 26 years; Geoff Affleck for his help in the production, publishing, and marketing of this book.. Lawrence Noyes for being such a strong, wise presence as a teacher and mentor in my life; Charles and Ava Berner for originating and developing this powerful work; Jeff Love for his writing—from which I borrowed—on the Enlightenment Intensive; Monica Piercy for intuiting that I was pregnant and about to give birth to this book; Doug Tyler, who supported me to give my first E.I.; Anjali Hill and Thomas Koven, my deep friends at the beginning of exploring this path; my mother, Irene Scott, for her indomitable spirit; my father, Marvin Scott, who taught me to be impeccable; my brothers Glenn, Jerry, and Gordon for opening up my "Clown Chakra;" my cousin Laverne for being there when I needed him; Ralph, my late dog, who showed me how to "just be what you are;" and all the truth seekers and truth guides that have walked the spiritual path and cast aside dogma to find the guru in themselves. Without your love, inspiration and presence, I wouldn't not have written this book.

WHO IS RUSSELL ALLEN SCOTT?

Russell is one of the new generation of no-dogma spiritual teachers. As the former owner of the Ecology Retreat Centre near Orangeville, Ontario, Canada, he pioneered programs in sustainable living and green building and received a broad experience in the many spiritual paths he encountered there. For over 35 years, through his one-on-one sessions and group retreats, he's been helping independent spiritual seekers awaken to their deeper meaning and purpose so they can walk in the beauty and honesty of who they really are with a clear mind and pure heart. He's also an accomplished singer/ songwriter who sometimes sings Country and Eastern songs. He gets great joy from witnessing people in his retreats fall off their seats in fits of laughter when they realize who they are.

RUSSELL'S SELF-DESCRIPTION

I'm just me.

I'm not this well-seasoned body, my neurotic personal history, or my awkward ego; although there are many times I really quite enjoy playing in my personality. Much to the chagrin of some religious folks, I do exist (I must exist in order to contemplate my existence, right?). Yet, I also do not exist, because no one thing defines me, not even the concept of existence. Now what I am, or my divine qualities, are quite another story: pure consciousness, bliss, universal love, infinite potential, cosmic intelligence, unlimited energy, non-dual awareness, everything, nothing, all the things in between, and more. You can find these attributes accentuated more or less in whatever spiritual book you study. Better yet, you'll find these qualities in the book of yourself.

I'm really the same as you; I'm just presenting myself uniquely and differently than you.

If I were to summarize it all, I'd say this:

I am you

You are me

The guru is us.

Made in the USA
Monee, IL
14 May 2022

96429144R00163